Sarah Greene Burger, R.N. [shown right]
received a B.A. from Connecticut College
and did her nurse's training at Radcliffe-
Massachusetts General Hospital School of
Nursing. Most of her nursing career has been
spent working with the elderly in nursing
homes. She is a consultant in nursing home affairs and works part-time as a registered nurse
in a D.C. nursing home. She is married to a
physician and is the mother of two daughters.

Martha D'Erasmo, R.N. graduated from St.
Luke's Hospital School of Nursing in New York.
She has worked in a variety of nursing situations in hospitals and nursing homes and has
been nursing director of a large extended-care
facility. She is presently nursing coordinator at a
Health Maintenance Organization. She lives
with her lawyer husband and two daughters in
suburban Maryland.

Jacket design by Donya Melanson Associates

A CONTINUUM BOOK
The Seabury Press
815 Second Avenue, New York, N.Y. 10017

Living in a Nursing Home

Living in a Nursing Home

A COMPLETE GUIDE
FOR RESIDENTS, THEIR FAMILIES
AND FRIENDS

Sarah Greene Burger, R.N.
Martha D'Erasmo, R.N.

A CONTINUUM BOOK
The Seabury Press, New York

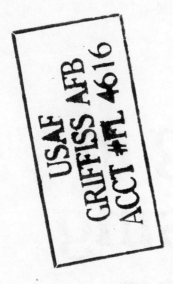
1976

The Seabury Press
815 Second Avenue, New York, New York 10017

Printed in the United States of America

Library of Congress Cataloging in Publication Data
Burger, Sarah Greene, 1935–
Living in a nursing home.
(A Continuum book)
Includes bibliographical references.
1. Nursing homes. 2. Nursing homes—United States.
I. D'Erasmo, Martha, 1939–   joint author. II. Title.
RA997.B87   362.6'15'0973   76-17890
ISBN 0-8164-9294-8

*To those special people living and working
in nursing homes, who have provided us with
the incentive to write this book and the
information upon which it is based.*

CONTENTS

PREFACE

What is a nursing home? It is a HOME. Whenever people think of health care institutions, they think of hospitals. Forget that. A nursing home provides some degree of nursing care in as home-like a setting as possible. Keep that firmly in mind. The relationship of family, friend, or resident to a nursing home will be very different from his or her relationship to a hospital.

As nurses who have both spent a number of years working with the elderly in nursing homes, we are continually struck by the confusion and fear families feel during and after admission of their relative to a home. Nursing homes have recently received bad publicity, some of it deserved. This increases the anger and guilt which families experience when considering placement in a nursing home.

But very often nursing home placement is the only solution to a particular set of problems. No magic formula can ease the decisions of when to enter, how to enter, or which institution to enter. Today, there are innumerable alternatives such as home care services provided by visiting nurse associations, day care centers for the elderly, homemaker services, church visiting programs, and others. These solutions should always be considered in depth before institutionalization.

This book is written to help those who are confronted with decisions about nursing home placement. It is directed toward both the families of elderly persons entering a home *and* toward the elderly person involved. Although written specifically about the elderly resident, the principles are applicable to people of any age entering a nursing home. We provide guides to follow before, during, and after admission to an institution. This book is also intended to aid professionals and para-professionals involved in any aspect of nursing home placement or care. These people include physicians, nurses, nursing assistants, orderlies, social workers, ministers, and many others. We can cite example upon example of the most grievous wrongs inadvertently perpetrated upon the elderly by well-meaning but misdirected people. Here is one instance of what we mean: A woman wanted to place her husband in a nursing home. We had a concerned chat about his health problems and daily routine. We asked one simple question:

"Have you discussed this move with your husband?"

"No," she replied, "both my doctor and his doctor advised that I tell him he was going to the hospital, not to a nursing home."

Imagine what this man, who was mentally sound although admittedly sometimes hazy, would suffer upon admission. The doctors were obviously trying to ease the wife's burden. However, it was a thoughtless suggestion. The husband would soon find he had left home forever. He would feel betrayed by the only people he knew he could trust: his wife and his doctor. He would be unprepared for the difficulties in adjusting to institutional life. A plan involving another person's life was made without his consent. Indeed this man was being sentenced.

Without passing judgment on the pros and cons of nursing homes in general or any one home in particular, it is a fact of modern society that they are one answer to the care of the older person. Families and residents should be aware of the responsibilities of a nursing home so they may demand the highest standards of care. At the same time they must be aware of their own continuing responsibilities, for nursing homes are often used as dumping grounds for the unwanted or forgotten in our society.

In this book we have used the term *nursing assistant* rather than *aide* or *nurses' aid* to describe those people providing the most intimate and basic care for the residents of nursing homes. In addition, we speak of the inhabitants of nursing homes as *residents* rather than *patients*. This will distinguish between those who reside in nursing homes and those who are hospitalized. In referring to residents we have used both *he* and *she*, at random throughout; this was done to avoid the awkward *he/she*, and unless specifically stated otherwise, all the information in this book applies to nursing home residents of both sexes. Finally, names of persons and places have been changed to protect privacy.

Living in a Nursing Home

ONE

The Story of Minnie Jones

Minnie and Jack Jones were a lucky couple who had married in their late twenties after adequate education and had no overwhelming financial burdens. They had lived almost a story-book existence with three children (a boy and two girls) born at comfortable two-year intervals. All three were now adults.

Now in their retirement years, Minnie and Jack lived comfortably in a small, new house, after selling the larger one nearby in which they had raised their family. The three children were married and lived relatively close to their parents. Weekends usually brought one family or another to visit with assorted grandchildren in tow. Mr. and Mrs. Jones enjoyed their visits mightily, but breathed a little sigh of relief when everyone departed and they had their cottage to themselves once more.

Jack retired about 10 years ago on what seemed an ample pension. This coupled with social security made a comfortable base and they lived a cozy if somewhat frugal existence. They had a savings account and medical insurance through the social security administration known as Medicare. This is an insurance program available to citizens 65 years of age and older. Jack and Minnie elected to take both Sections A and B of the offered coverage. Section A covers hospital costs and Section B some doctors' fees and services. Also included are some pharmacy and health care items.

They received an attractive booklet along with their health care cards. It was fairly easy to read and spelled out coverage including 90 hospital days, and 100 days of "extended care coverage." The clerk at the Social Security Office explained that extended care applied to nursing home care but gave no further details.

Minnie and Jack did not read carefully enough to notice the phrase "up to 90 hospital days," and were blissfully unaware that very few people actually qualify for such extensive care. Every facility, nursing home or hospital, that participates in Medicare has a committee which must pass on the suitability of continuing benefits for each patient. Under Medicare guidelines many are disqualified for benefits within a few days. Even if the committee does extend benefits, the claim is reviewed at Medicare regional offices where it may be disallowed by the reviewer. There is an appeal process, but comprehending and dealing with bureaucratic procedures is difficult enough for everyone and especially so if one is old and sick.

Jack and Minnie had seldom visited doctors' offices even as they grew older. Jack was finally driven to seek medical care when a persistent chest discomfort and difficulty in sleeping frightened him and Minnie. He was pleasantly surprised by the attitude and manner of his young physician. Jack was quickly diagnosed as having mild chronic heart failure and placed on medication. He took his medicine faithfully and kept his routine doctor's appointments.

Partly because of the careful, realistic medical monitoring he received in his later years, Jack's death at the age of 78 was peaceful and dignified. He died in his favorite easy chair while watching the evening news.

Everyone was deeply saddened but they were also

amazed at Minnie's ability to bring loving realism to the situation.

"After all," she said, "he died here at home with me. That is as it should be."

After Jack's death, the family was in a quandary. What would be best for Minnie? At this point she took matters into her own hands. She announced to the family that the only sensible decision was for her to stay right where she was. After all, the house was small. Neighbors were close and she had a phone. With a certain reluctance, laced with relief, her children agreed.

Her son John went over her finances and found that she had a small but apparently ample income for a comfortable, if simple, life. In a family conference they agreed that if something unexpectedly large came up, like an increased tax assessment, they would help her.

Things went along calmly for the next few years, better, in fact, than any of them had anticipated. All of the children were involved with their own families. But they made a point to call her daily. And there were always visits back and forth on weekends. Minnie never told her children of her private feelings during this time. First, there was the constant loneliness. It was not an acute feeling, but rather a dull emptiness that would have been hard for her to put into words. It was the feeling that another human being who had come to be almost an extension of herself was gone; a presence constant for years was now missing.

The second change she was only dimly aware of. Minnie was a woman of strong habits which prevailed even now that she was alone. She continued to rise, dress, comb her hair, straighten her house, and prepare her food, as she had always done. But now she was often preoccupied while working with thoughts about her past. She would relive an event or conversation word for word. These memories occupied much more time than she realized and for some reason gave her great comfort. Minnie would have been very surprised to learn that this introspective memory searching is called "life review" by some. It is often called the final life task, a reappraisal of worth and redefinition of one's purpose in life. A satisfying old age occurs when a person's life review reveals a life that was good for this individual. For Minnie, luckily, this was the case and from this she derived comfort and consolation.

She was also fortunate because her family stayed in close touch. Her daughter took her shopping weekly and all the children and grandchildren called her often. She had friends and interested neighbors who maintained constant contact.

Minnie's physical status was declining slowly. Her attention was becoming less acute. Her arthritis, an old companion, was causing her to move more slowly and drop things frequently. As this annoyed her, others called the least possible attention to it.

On a chilly, fall morning, Minnie awoke earlier than usual with the ever-present arthritis more than usually painful. She rose slowly and went to the kitchen to put on water for tea. While she waited for it to boil she decided a warm bath might relieve her aching joints.

After drawing the bath she got carefully into the steamy water, and did indeed feel welcome relief from the pain. As she was standing to get out of the tub she suddenly smelled something burning. "The tea pot! I forgot all about it," she exclaimed, and tried to move quickly. What happened next was not quite clear but she probably caught her foot on the towel or rug. She fell heavily to the floor. She was stunned and a little dizzy. After lying still a few moments she tried to get up but an excruciating pain tore through her left hip and leg. Mercifully, she lost consciousness.

Meanwhile, her middle-aged next-door neighbor appeared at the kitchen door. For some time she had made a point of checking on Minnie every day. She knocked several times and finally glanced in the window. The pot was smoking and she was alarmed. Luckily she knew that an extra key to the house was kept in a small utility shed. She went in, turned off the stove, and found Minnie in the bathroom.

She covered her with a blanket, phoned the rescue squad, and finally found one daughter's phone number in a small address book near the phone. Monica, the older daughter, was at home and rushed to the emergency room of the local hospital. From there she phoned her brother and sister.

The next few days were a blur for Minnie Jones. First, she was suffering from shock due to the trauma of the fall, lying cold and wet for half an hour, and the pain. Her blood pressure had dropped, her pulse speeded up and she slipped in and out of consciousness. This condition was handled effectively and efficiently by the competent emergency room team.

Additionally, and more important to Minnie herself, she had become a "case" or a "problem" rather than a person in her own right. People and events whirled around her. Decisions were made and things done about which she was only cursorily consulted.

When Monica arrived at the hospital she was greeted with a thousand questions. The admitting clerk and the surgeon asked everything from "Does your mother have any allergies?" to "Where is her Medicare card?" The family was poorly prepared for this emergency. Monica had to rack her brain to answer and had to ask her sister Mary to go to Mrs. Jones' house to find the

Medicare card (which was tucked in a bureau drawer and took a long time to find). The number of forms and questions was amazing, and Monica had a blazing headache before she even saw her mother. This was particularly sad because Minnie badly needed reassurance and hand holding. But the mainstream of hospital life moved so quickly that there was never a quiet, free moment for Mary or Monica to comfort her.

The physicians and nurses were thorough, professional, and kindly, but in an offhand manner. Such situations are everyday occurrences for them and things were handled quickly. An orthopedic surgeon was called. He reviewed her x-rays and general physical condition and advised surgery to insert a steel plate to hold her badly shattered hip together. The children were worried but the surgeon was reassuring. Mrs. Jones had trouble understanding. The intern had noted that she appeared confused. It was more likely that, after all she had endured, her reactions were slowed and that the speed of the questioning was too fast for her.

John reluctantly signed the surgical consent and a variety of things, some painful, some frightening, were done to Minnie. Blood was drawn from her arm; a catheter to drain urine was inserted into her bladder; intravenous fluids were started in her veins and intramuscular injections to ease pain and facilitate anesthesia were given. She was wheeled off to surgery in a painful haze with no clear idea of where she was going or why. After surgery she was taken to a recovery room and later, after awakening, was taken to her hospital room.

Minnie's first few hospital days were unhappy for her and her children. She couldn't seem to "get her bearings," or understand what had happened or where

she was. Naturally she was upset and called out, re-
sisted care, and became generally disruptive. Her children, who had never seen her anything but neat, col-
lected, and in control of herself, were upset and didn't
know what to do. They responded by asking many
anxious questions of the nurses and aides. Because of
the family's inexperience, they caused resentment
among many aides and some nurses, who felt their
competence was being questioned. The doctor never
seemed to make his rounds while they were visiting
and the interns and resident physicians always seemed
extremely busy. The three families felt abandoned and
unable to cope, and they transferred much of their
unspoken anxiety to Minnie.

In about a week Minnie began to improve. She was
lifted out of the bed daily. Her daughters fixed her
hair and fussed over her. They still didn't understand
what had happened but were relieved to see her better.

Two weeks after surgery, the doctor announced to
Minnie's shocked family that she would be discharged
in a few days. The hospital's "Utilization Review Committee" (the professional group that meets and decides
whether each patient covered by Medicare benefits is
still in need of hospitalization and requires further
benefits) had met and decided that Mrs. Jones was no
longer in need of acute hospital care and her Medicare
benefits would cease as of three days hence.

The children were beside themselves, especially since
the doctor seemed a little vague about what could be
done. He did refer them to the hospital social worker's
office. John, Mary, and Monica made an appointment
with Miss Smith for that same afternoon.

When they entered her office the three anxious people were reassured by Miss Smith's pleasant smile and
no-nonsense attitude. As they explained their predica-

ment she nodded and gently explained that this same problem occurred hundreds of times a year.

She started by spelling out their alternatives carefully. These were:

(1) To take Minnie back to her own home and hire full-time help to care for her until she recovered.

(2) To take her to one of their own homes and probably hire part-time help.

(3) To place her in a nursing home.

As they talked and worked things out with the social worker it became apparent that the first alternative was not practical. Full-time, live-in help is extremely hard to find and extremely expensive. It costs on an average $40 per day. This amounts to $16,000 per year when you include overtime pay for holidays and weekends. The companion has little supervision and problems arise with frightening frequency. The second was impossible because of work schedules and some pre-existing medical problems in each child's home. None of the children had a house large enough to have their mother live with them permanently. They all worked, so Minnie would be alone part of every weekday.

As they reluctantly came to the third choice, "nursing home placement," their concern grew.

"Miss Smith, we know nothing about these places," explained John.

"We've all read horrible stories about them. Can we really send our mother to a nursing home?"

Miss Smith sighed.

"I understand your concern. Yes, I think your mother can be comfortably placed in a home, if we follow certain steps and are careful and thorough. We have to look at this from several viewpoints. We must consider location, the level of care, financial aspects, and bed availability in the nursing homes in this area.

"Since your mother is covered by Medicare, you will want to choose a Medicare certified facility. Now, I am going to be blunt. What is your financial situation? Can you afford to help your mother pay her way?"

John answered, "That shouldn't be necessary, with her widow's pension and social security, plus Medicare benefits."

Miss Smith explained that care at many homes with all expenses included can cost $1,000 a month or more. The Medicare situation in nursing homes is the same as in hospitals. They also have committees that must meet stringent care certification standards. She added that Mrs. Jones' benefits might terminate in a few weeks and the family would face the same situation all over again.

All three looked grim. Monica finally said, "The truth is, that none of us can afford a large monthly financial drain. If a one-time situation came up we could pool our resources and handle it, but we couldn't if it were continuing."

"Mother does have some savings," said John. "But I hate to see her deplete them when we don't know what may come next!"

"What does the doctor say about your mother's prognosis?" asked Miss Smith.

"He's pretty vague, says we'll have to wait and see how she does and what x-rays show in the next months."

After much discussion they decided to try for a bed in a nursing home located about equidistant from John, Mary, and Monica. It was qualified to accept Medicare patients and was well thought of in the community. The building was fairly new, pleasant and sunny, with large windows and porches. While Minnie's coverage lasted it was free. But should cost revert to them it would amount to about $1,000 per month.

They decided to hope for the best from Medicare and should that cease, to dip into Minnie's savings. But they were sure that she would soon be better and ready to return home. They did, however, briefly discuss selling Minnie's house if there were no other choice.

When Miss Smith called Sunnydale Home she found that there was an available bed, and that Mrs. Jones could be admitted the next day.

Because Minnie had been so sick her children had not wanted to disturb her and had not told her their plans. Imagine her surprise when they came to her room and announced that tomorrow she would be moved to Sunnydale Nursing Home. She became querulous and said she didn't see any sense to that; she was doing fine where she was. She had heard horrible things about those places and she didn't want to go!

When the ambulance arrived Monica rode with Minnie to Sunnydale. Their first impression was pleasant. It was a bright sunny day. The rooms were cheerful, the nurse pleasant. The sight of some old, bewildered persons tied into their wheelchairs disturbed them but Monica quickly dismissed them as "nothing like mother" and averted her eyes.

Minnie was stoically silent as she was placed in bed and managed a wan smile for the nurse. Her things were hung in the closet or put in drawers. Minnie looked shocked when the nurse's aide told her this was her new home, but said nothing. Monica, needing some reassurance herself, did more bustling about than was necessary.

Lunch came and Minnie ate very little but seemed more cheerful. Monica went to the business office again to fill out myriad forms, to present her mother's

Medicare card, and to answer questions. Finally she thankfully left for home.

Some strange things happened during the next few weeks. On the surface Mrs. Jones seemed relatively content. She was eating well, was up in a chair daily, and was evaluated by the physical therapist, who gave her some mild strengthening arm and leg exercises, hoping she might learn to walk again.

When Mary, Monica, and John visited she would say, "Now, don't worry about me, everything's fine," and in the same breath speak of one aide or another as being "a little mean." She might say, "Isn't it too bad that Miss Randall, my night nurse, stole my pink gown." Her family was confused when the pink gown turned up in her drawer, but when they looked up the aide who had been accused of meanness, they found her really abrupt. She had an unpleasant expression, so they could easily understand their mother's reaction.

Minnie was adjusting to this rapid change in her life. She had gone from a state of independence to one of almost childlike dependence in the space of a few weeks. She was angry and hurt at all that had happened and more than a little panicky. Her children had started treating her more like a child than a responsible adult and she didn't know how to react. Their treatment of her had convinced her that she would never be well. She was sure they were hiding vital facts. She was lashing out in anger at the most obvious of her problems, the nursing home where she didn't want to be. She hadn't meant to lie about the gown, but had angrily convinced herself it had been stolen. The nursing assistants were members of a minority group against which she had an ingrained prejudice, so she unconsciously telegraphed her fear and dislike. These aides had had minimal training and none to help them cope with prejudice. They were surly through ignorance rather than design.

Minnie's family were still unsure how to handle the situation. They were unfamiliar with the nursing home hierarchy and did not know to whom to take their problems. They eventually found their way to Minnie's floor supervisor who helped them.

In a few weeks Minnie's hip was x-rayed again. The doctor told John that Minnie's chances for recovery were slim. Her bones were extremely osteoporotic (that is, showed decreased bone mass due to lower mineral and protein components), and he feared that even with the plate the hip would refracture should she put weight on it.

The family called a conference. They decided not to tell Minnie the truth. They would say she needed a little more time to heal and more exercises. The doctor said she could stand a little in the physical therapy department, but only on her good leg. They decided to tell her that standing was a prelude to walking.

When they told her, Mrs. Jones looked at them sharply. When she started to ask pointed questions they quickly shut her off. Minnie Jones was no fool. She had raised these people to adulthood. She knew intimately their various facial gestures and the mannerisms that told her they were not telling the truth. She realized that *she would never leave this place* and was surprised by the depth of her anger and despair. She decided, however, to go along with the game. The daily routines continued but something almost imperceptible was happening. Minnie's spirit was slipping.

After the x-ray report and doctor's note had been entered on the chart, Minnie became ineligible for further Medicare benefits at the nursing home.

John got a form letter notifying him that Minnie's benefits would end in three days. This time the shock was less great and Miss Smith's good preparation helped.

Since Minnie's fall John, Mary, and Monica had been shielding her from reality and from making decisions. While they had done so with the best of intentions, they had done themselves and their mother a disservice. Minnie could have handled reality much better than sugarcoated half-truths.

Now they were in a quandary. John would need a power of attorney to enable him to use Minnie's bank account to pay for her care. Also, in the back of all of their minds was the idea that they might have to sell her house. None of them wanted to tell her that.

There was no way out but to consult her directly. Minnie seemed relieved rather than upset, readily signed the power of attorney, but balked at doing anything positive about selling the house.

"Let's wait a bit," she said. "My savings will carry me awhile and maybe by then I'll be ready to leave here and go back home."

Things went calmly for the next few months but Minnie was losing ground. Her interest in hygiene and in her appearance decreased and she avoided going to physical therapy. The night nurses had noted that sometimes in the middle of the night she would waken, confused about where she was and what she was doing there. One horrible night she was confused and tried to climb out of bed. She couldn't seem to get words together to explain that she was just going to the bathroom and to check on John, and what was this strange girl doing in her home anyway? By morning it was all like a bad dream and she couldn't understand what had possessed her. Unknown to her, her physician entered an order on her chart for "light restraints as necessary."

Minnie's savings were rapidly melting away and her physical condition was such that it seemed apparent she must stay where she was. Selling the house became essential, and John put it on the market without mentioning it to his mother. The little home sold quickly. Mary and Monica cried as they sorted their mother's possessions.

Minnie's physical and mental changes were daily becoming more apparent. She seemed smaller than before. Her skin was loose on her frame, wrinkled and dry to the touch. Her attention span was considerably shortened. She dozed daily while sitting in her wheelchair and slept only sporadically at night. While in her wheelchair she had one of those hateful restraints and at night another which allowed her to turn but kept her in bed.

She asked about her home and finances now and again and always got evasive answers. After a while she stopped asking.

During her second winter at the home Minnie developed pneumonia. She was promptly treated with antibiotics, and given intravenous feeding to supplement food and fluids she could take by mouth. She was placed on a careful turning schedule. Every two hours her position was changed to facilitate optimal lung expansion and prevent bed sores. Oxygen was administered to help her breathe. Her family, notified of her condition, quickly arrived. They were shocked and disturbed by what they saw.

The crucial decision was whether to keep her where she was or remove her to a hospital. After a long conference with her doctor and nursing supervisor, they agreed not to put her through the trauma and fear of moving.

Her daughters and son took turns sitting by her bed. While she didn't acknowledge their presence, everyone agreed she seemed less restless when one of them was present. They were all uneasy and uncomfortable during those long hours. This had been a loving and sharing family. Nevertheless, they were poorly prepared to help their mother. They all wanted to do something for her. They welcomed chances to help the nurse turn her. But what Minnie probably needed was much more difficult to give—quiet hand holding and support were what she most needed.

Minnie died at 3:00 A.M. on the morning of the third day. Her daughter Mary was dozing by her bed and realized immediately that her mother had died.

The feeling of the children, their spouses and grandchildren was one of grief mixed with relief.

What could this family have done to alter the course of things? Which happenings were inevitable? What were the good and bad aspects of their nursing home experience? We don't have all the answers, but in the following chapters we will tell you what our experience and research have taught us about an increasingly common family problem. There are no pat answers or easy formulae for nursing home placement, but the more knowledge you have and support you can give when faced with this decision, the more realistic and compassionate you can be.

TWO

Who Are the Elderly in Our Nursing Homes?

Let us backtrack a few steps and find out just who is living in nursing homes today and how they came to be there. Is Minnie Jones typical of the national nursing home population? What is normal in the aging process? What is abnormal, or attributable to disease? And, what medical, economic, and social changes account for the increased use of nursing homes?

In order to describe the nursing home residents over the age of 65, we must first describe what is normal in the aging process. Minnie Jones' story is typical. Aging is a normal part of the life cycle of birth, growth, and death. It is startling to realize that in some respects physical maturity is reached in the early years between ages 15 and 17 for women and between 17 and 19 for men. Thereafter our bodies deteriorate progressively.

The rate of this process varies greatly among individuals. This variation often produces a state in which physical and chronological age do not seem to coincide perfectly. We all know people who age faster or more slowly than we expect. Accepting these variations, let us consider the major external and internal bodily changes. Remember, we are not discussing disease but rather the normal aging process. Each change or loss requires a corresponding adjustment in the adult's lifestyle.

We will begin with the skin. This body organ be-

comes dry and wrinkled because the sweat and seba-
cious glands function less effectively. Its elasticity diminishes, causing enormous areas of discoloration
when bruised. As the circulation of the blood to the
skin slows, the cold is felt more readily and requires
older people to use a sweater or shawl. Also, when
broken, the skin may be more susceptible to infection.
Other characteristics of normal aging are apparent in
the face. The teeth may begin to drop out. Simone de
Beauvoir has described this process aptly in her book,
The Coming of Age:

> The loss of teeth brings about a shortening of the lower
> part of the face, so that the nose, lengthened vertically by
> the atrophy (wasting away) of elastic tissues, comes nearer
> to the chin. The growth of skin in the aged causes a thick-
> ening of the eyelids, while at the same time hollows appear
> beneath the eyes. The upper lip becomes thinner. The
> lobe of the ear increases in size.[1]

What effect do you suppose such changes have on
the self-esteem of the older person in our society?
Other changes occur for as-yet-unknown reasons. The
hair whitens, thins, and is redistributed, as on the chins
of women. Changes in the bone structure also contribute to a change in appearance in the older person.
What are these changes and what effect do they have
on a person's lifestyle?

As an individual becomes older the actual bone mass
decreases as much as ten percent after the age of 45.
This process begins in the spine, pelvis, and long bones
of the legs and arms. The spinal discs compress, making the vertebrae (backbone) closer together, causing
the bowed back of the older person. Between 45 and
85 years of age a man's chest measurements decrease
by 10 centimeters (about 4 inches) and a woman's by as

much as 15 centimeters (or 6 inches).[2] In addition the bones become more porous (less dense) and lose elasticity. Therefore, they become more brittle. There may be changes in the bones which cause new stresses. For instance, the angle of the neck or top of the femur (leg bone) where it attaches to the rest of the bone changes just enough to make fractures much more common.

This, of course, is exactly what happened to Mrs. Jones. The elderly person must constantly adjust not only to a different appearance but also a more vulnerable constitution. Just one example will illustrate the difficulties caused by changes in the leg bone. Think, for a minute, what it is like for Minnie Jones to take a bus somewhere. Bus steps are very high, as are the steps of trains. Getting on and off a bus can cause an enormous jolt against which older people must constantly guard. Travel can become so difficult that the elderly person becomes a recluse and isolation may follow.

We should consider what happens to the inner systems of the body and what adjustments must occur to cope with these changes. Does it shock you that several thousand brain cells die each day? There are about half as many cells in the frontal area of the brain at the age of 80 as at the age of 40. The weight of the brain is cut in half. Fortunately, we have an enormous reserve capacity in the brain which enables us to continue functioning fairly steadily. Add to this a decrease in blood circulation to the brain caused by less efficient functioning of the heart and decreased elasticity of the blood vessels. It is a credit to our bodies that they adjust to such changes so magnificently. The quality of the five senses (hearing, smell, taste, sight, touch) diminishes with age because of the decreased number of cells in these systems. Hearing decreases first in the higher frequencies and then in the lower conversational tones. The older person has trouble keeping in touch with his surroundings. Block your ears with a muffler for a period of time and you will see how many touchstones of life are lost: the arrival of a car in the driveway, the chime of a clock, birds signalling the arrival of daybreak. There are thousands of sounds in our daily life which help to keep us oriented.

An acute sense of smell helps to prevent accidents, especially in the home. Suppose a gas stove is turned on but remains unlighted. An older person might not smell the leaking gas until too late. Fire poses another problem for people with a diminished sense of smell.

Vision or sight begins to decrease at age twenty. At first the vision may be slightly less acute. The elasticity of the lens of the eye decreases, reducing the visual fields, or the amount one can see. Adaptation of the eye to light and dark becomes much slower. Over the years the peripheral or side vision may fade. Imagine crossing a city street without the proper hearing or vision! It is no wonder older people feel safer at home and often choose not to cope with unfamiliar surroundings. They have reason to be uneasy and insecure.

The fifth sense, touch, also may diminish in intensity. Suppose Minnie Jones had put her hand on the hot pan on the stove. She might not have felt the pain quite as acutely as in her younger days. In addition she would have been slower to pull back her hand from the hot pot. The musculature of the elderly person is slower and less precise. Long periods of muscle effort are less easily sustained. The rapid voluntary movements needed to draw back from a hot stove are not performed as quickly. It can be difficult to make corrective movements, as it was for Minnie Jones to recover her stability once her balance was upset. The complications are compounded for an elderly person who for any reason becomes inactive. He suffers a greater loss of muscle power than a younger person. Regaining the lost musculature is also much slower. After Mrs. Jones's hip had been set and was mending nicely, she still remained quite weak. Younger members of the family forgot this, and their expectations were too high.

As taste and smell diminish, food becomes less appetizing. A downward cycle of nutrition may result. As the elderly become less physically active, their appetites may also diminish. They may lose interest in eating alone. If a person eats too little or improperly, mental confusion results and meals may be still more neglected. In addition, the entire digestive system undergoes changes which require new eating habits and disturb elimination patterns. A vicious cycle ensues. Possibly Minnie Jones experienced this. Food passes through the stomach and into the bowel. In the older person the bowel may be sluggish, causing an uncomfortable full feeling and constipation. An increased intake of fruits, vegetables, and roughage may be necessary.

Another change which causes a problem for the older person is that of bladder control. As the muscles of the bladder become less efficient the older person may experience some dribbling. This can be horrifying and can impose drastic changes in one's lifestyle. Would you want to go to a movie if you thought you were going to wet your pants even slightly? This can be a devastating experience.

We have established, then, a baseline of bodily changes normal to the process of aging. We have barely begun to describe their effect on everyday life. These facts alone could well explain why one person in five over the age of 65 years will spend some time in a nursing home before he or she dies. There are, however, other factors which have forced Minnie Jones and over a million people like her into nursing homes for periods averaging one and one-half to three years.

Medical science has served us well in the prolonging of life. The median age of nursing home residents is 81 years, and the majority are women.[3] This, coupled with a decrease in fertility due to birth control, has changed the population's age distribution dramatically. Consider these facts: in 1850 in the United States, only 2.5% of the population was over 65; by 1900 this figure had increased to 4.1%. But today, 10% of our population, or over 20 million persons, are over 65. This number may increase to 28 million by the year 2000.[4] These figures represent, in part, medical advances which have changed disease patterns in the United States. Because people live longer, the amount of chronic long-term illness requiring institutional care has increased. Bacterial pneumonia used to be called the friend of the old, but that cause of quick death has decreased and people live to be burdened by other more debilitating diseases. Heart disease, although its mortality (death) rate has decreased in the last twenty years, is now the leading cause of death. Other causes of death are cancer (on the increase), cerebrovascular disease (stroke), accidents, and finally influenza and pneumonia, in that order.[5]

With these figures in mind, let us examine some socio-economic factors which have contributed to a dislocation of the older Americans. This dislocation, in turn, has created a greater dependency on institutionalization in later life. Industrialization has changed a primarily rural society to an urban one. In 1800 roughly 93% of the population lived in rural areas. By

1900 this figure had changed to 40%, and by 1970 to 27%. Conversely, 73% of the population were living in urban areas by 1970.[6] How did a change from rural to urban living affect the family? In a rural setting more than one generation lived together on the same land and often under the same roof. A farm was passed from father to son. Everyone who was physically able to work did so. Older people had a special place in the home. Experience had taught them how to cope with the natural hazards of agrarian survival, they were honored and respected for their knowledge, and this information was passed to succeeding generations. Even when they were confined to the home, there was a special place for the elderly. For instance, an important relationship between grandparent and grandchild often existed, and balance of discipline and warmth often characterized the relationship.

Today we see a very different pattern. Only 4% of our population is required to produce the food for the other 96%. Non-rural people are primarily involved in industry. The working life of the population is shortened. A person retires somewhere between the ages of 62 and 70, depending on the health of the individual, and the type of work. In 1967, only 21% of the population age 65 or over reported earnings from wages or self-employment. Those aged 65–72 were three times as likely to be wage earners as those 73 years or older. Thus we may conclude that 79% of the population over 65 is retired.[7]

What is the effect of retirement on our population over 65? Upon retirement one often feels actual loss of status in the family and in society, so that "the same society which may compel retirement or label a person 'too old' to get a job somehow rejects the person who does not produce." [8] The extended family no longer exists, reducing the importance of the elderly in the family structure and removing the protected concerned environment it once afforded. Certainly Mrs. Jones fits this social pattern. Even though her family were concerned for her health and safety, she was living alone and physically apart from her children. Her grandchildren, though important to her and loved, were not her responsibility. In a way she was an outsider to the second and third generations. Her friends, also elderly, were her most valuable daily contacts.

What are the economic factors which accentuate the dislocation for the elderly? Upward mobility is basic to American values. Acquiring an education is one method of achieving this goal. Once gained, education often leaves an unbridgeable gap between generations.

Job mobility separates the generations. Geographic mobility is illustrated by the fact that 35% of the male work force between the ages of 20 and 64 changed state residence between 1965 and 1970.[9] Even when two or more generations of the same family live in the same geographic area, the housing patterns of today—apartments or small single family dwellings—make accommodating an elderly family member difficult. Although Minnie Jones' family lived fairly close to her, her children were in no position to take her into their homes on a permanent basis. They did a lot of soul-searching about this and felt very guilty about their inability to have her live with them. The elderly in our population, then, are cut off from their families and society by factors over which they have no control.

And if the elderly person is an immigrant, who has clung to his or her ethnic culture, the isolation may be even more pronounced. An immigrant may never learn English, yet his children may become completely assimilated, discarding every vestige of their native heritage.

Accentuating these factors, which cause isolation among the elderly, is the obvious stress on youthfulness in the United States. We are exhorted daily by the media about the wonders of being young. We are told to eat certain foods to remain young, to apply special cosmetics to look young, and even to live in certain places to be young. It has been noted about the older population that ". . . most often their discontent with themselves was a reflection of the non-accepting attitudes of people about them. Ours is a youth centered culture. We still think it is a great compliment to say that a person doesn't look his age. The older person who judges himself—his appearance, strength, stamina, speed—by prevailing cultural standards is bound to suffer frustrations." [10]

Over one million of these people spend some time, or end their days, in some form of nursing home. There has been a 47% increase in the number of people in nursing homes since 1964.[11] Our government responded to the need for long-term care with passage of Medicare-Medicaid (titles 18, 19 of the Social Security Act) in 1965; thus, the legislation is quite recent. Other needs of the elderly population have been met through a variety of legislation establishing such aids as: Old Age Assistance, maintenance payments, foster grandparent program, and community planning and services. Finally, legislation directly affecting the nursing home industry was passed in the form of the Hospital Medical Facilities Construction, the Hill-Burton program, and Nursing Home Mortgage Insurance.

Nursing home facilities increased 140% between 1960 and 1970.[12]

There are many Minnie Joneses who have accommodated successfully to the normal changes of aging, and yet will live long enough to be overcome by some debilitating disease. Her fellow nursing-home residents will have multiple infirmities ranging from loss of hearing to terminal cancer or heart disease. She will find that the older the resident, the greater the number of infirmities he or she will have. Residents over the age of 85 have an average of 3.8 chronic (long-term) conditions per person, whereas residents between the ages of 65 and 74 have only 3.2 such conditions per person. Women have a slightly higher number of chronic diseases than men. These conditions necessarily restrict the mobility of the elderly. More than 25% of the residents over 65 in nursing homes are confined to bed or are up in a chair for only short periods of time. Women are more likely to be confined to bed than men. Minnie will find that the condition of residents in her nursing home, as in others across the country, ranges from complete mobility, to walking with assistance, or independence with the use of a wheelchair.[13] In the total nursing home population over 65, about 32% use wheelchairs and 12% use a walker. 40% of the population requires eyeglasses. The use of such aids increases as a resident becomes older.[14]

Even under the most fortunate circumstances, today's world is harsh on our more than 20 million elderly citizens. Mrs. Jones did not face many of the burdens which are especially defeating to her age group, such as lack of living relatives, poverty, language barriers, sex discrimination, or racial discrimination. Yet, Mrs. Jones' situation was still very difficult to solve.

There should have been a way to build on her strengths and preserve her dignity as a person.

How could the harshness of her last months have been ameliorated? We shall address this problem in the ensuing chapters.

THREE

Shopping for a Nursing Home

One of the most difficult times anyone faces comes after the final hard decision that a nursing home is the only place for a relative or friend. At this moment great support is necessary for both the patient and those responsible for reaching the decision with him.

Once this difficult decision has been made, there are a number of facts and options to consider. It is easiest to sit down and systematically list and check them off one by one.

The following outline can be enlarged upon, depending on your personal wishes. It is intended as a guideline for fact-gathering and decision-making. Items 1–4 are for information gathering—these are things you need to know or think about before any sensible placement decision can be reached. Item 5 shows you how you can personally evaluate any nursing home you visit.

1. **Patient's present mental and physical status**
   —Physician
   —If hospitalized—nurses, aides, orderlies
   —If homebound—neighbors
   —Friends and relatives
2. **Cold Facts**
   —Finances
   —Insurance Benefits
   —Types of available and adequate facilities
   —Applicable medical coverage

3. **Medical Facts and Prognosis**
   —Improvement expected?
   —Short- or long-term placement; anticipated time of placement
   —Physician's willingness to visit patient during nursing home placement
   —Special services for this patient
   —Special equipment for this patient
4. **Social and Aesthetic Facts**
   Geography
   —Patient's preference
   —Friend and relative preference
   (a) Transportation available for visitors to reach patient?
   —Maintenance of patient's usual activities and habits (see Chapter 4)
   —Church affiliations (patient's)
   —Single or double room
5. **Actual Inspection**
   —Free admittance (any locked doors?)
   —License status
   —Type of facility
   —Odor
   —Attitude
   —Bathroom and bathing facilities
   —Hidden costs
   —Dining facilities and patient's response
   —Noise level

This outline is purposely simple and short. As we work through it you'll see how many facts emerge from these few basic questions.

It is *essential* for the people carrying out this procedure to stay as objective as possible. There are just too many small details to consider to have your concentration destroyed by being distraught.

The first rule of thumb is DON'T PANIC. Sit back,

gather everyone around you who is involved and open up discussion. The person who is most often left out of the decision-making process is the very one who should be consulted first—the patient!

How much happier Minnie would have been had her children been open with her. She had been a sensible woman all her life. It would not have been unreasonable to assume her common sense would assert itself again.

We can think of no instance where the patient should not be consulted regarding nursing home placement. Even if you find yourself in that tragic situation in which a friend or relative has been rendered seemingly non-comprehending due to illness or accident, tell him anyway what's going on. Medical science still knows too little about coma. It is entirely possible the person is able to hear and assimilate the information even though he can express nothing. Even if the patient appears senile or very confused, give a complete explanation.

We will now go through the outline step by step with tips on how to proceed.

I. Patient's Present Mental and Physical Status

In the majority of cases the decision to seek nursing home placement is precipitated by some personal emergency or catastrophe. The facts regarding this person may have been unalterably changed in the space of a few days. You simply cannot proceed logically in reaching a sensible decision if you don't know the facts.

Your doctor is an essential member of this team. Get him to spell out to you as far as he is able the patient's immediate and future needs. Remember, though, that no one can say with absolute certainty what the future will be. You can, however, reasonably expect him to give you some hard medical facts and information about the level of care he feels the patient needs. You can also ask him his opinion of the nursing homes in the area.

You will also need to find out whether he will continue to visit and care for the patient after nursing home placement. Habits and practices vary widely from place to place. Some homes have staff physicians who follow all patients admitted. Others expect private doctors to visit patients there. Go over this very carefully with both your physician and the nursing home and be sure you have a clear understanding of what will happen.

If the person has been hospitalized, speak directly to those nursing assistants and orderlies who have been giving direct care. Find out from them how independent your friend or relative is presently. If you are dealing with a situation in which an older person is at home but increasingly infirm, talk to neighbors and local storekeepers, etc., with whom he has fairly frequent contact. Many times these people have important information to share that can give you a more realistic picture of how this person has been managing. Most adults try to protect their own independence. Many older people successfully hide vital facts regarding sight, falls, confused disorders, etc., from younger relatives and friends because they fear losing this independence. It often takes a more peripheral acquaintance to point out the real truth of a situation.

Last but not least, speak with as many friends and relatives of the patient as have had fairly frequent contact with him and elicit their ideas and feelings. One word of caution here, however—in some families this type of discussion can lead to loud voices and serious dissension. But this will probably occur anyway and it is wiser to get it out of the way before, rather than after, the fact. If a family finds itself simply unable to reach a mutually acceptable decision, then an outside third party, such as a trusted doctor, nurse, social worker, or clergyman should be brought in to help.

II. Cold Facts

All of the good intentions and loving care in the world can be completely useless if inadequate attention is given to cold realities. What can we pay for and what is available?

The first necessity is to ascertain the patient's present resources and expenses. You will need to know not only the income but the value of real property, savings accounts, bonds, etc. You will also have to explore the family's financial situation. Is this a family where financial help can reasonably be expected on a long-term basis? These are all difficult questions. Fact gathering on other people's finances is always a thankless task.

While you are getting this information you will also need to explore the patient's particular insurance benefits. Most private medical insurances do not cover nursing home care. But do not assume this to be the case. Read the fine print of the contract carefully and if you are confused contact the company and get an opinion *in writing*.

Medicare, the government sponsored insurance through social security, is available to those 65 years of age and older for a relatively nominal sum. This insurance does have nursing home coverage in a "Catch 22" sort of way. It is possible, but improbable, for coverage to be provided for up to 100 days after spending three or more days hospitalized.

Each Medicare certified nursing home is required by law to maintain a "Utilization Review" committee. The function of this group is to pass on whether a patient is eligible for continued coverage under Medicare guidelines. As a rule of thumb, ask the question: (1) Is this a condition from which this person has any recovery potential or (2) Has a plateau been reached from which upward change is impossible or unlikely? In the latter case, Medicare benefits generally cease.

Medicaid is the companion insurance equivalent of welfare for those whose income falls under $2,500.00. There should be no shame attached to the use of Medicaid funds. Both Medicare and Medicaid practice what must be termed "adverse selection." For instance, if a patient is admitted to a nursing home following serious illness or accident and quickly reaches recovery potential due to excellent care, he is dropped (or in the case of Medicaid payment decreased to a lower figure) as no longer requiring "skilled care." However, if he is not followed quite as closely as necessary and develops a decubitus ulcer (bedsore) from lack of adequate turning, becomes moderately dehydrated because fluids aren't offered and encouraged often enough, and requires a catheter for urinary incontinence, largely from not being walked to the bathroom frequently enough, he is deemed in need of skilled care to repair those problems and payment continues.

There are several private insurances that cover nursing home care and some prepaid medical practices have fairly liberal benefits. Be certain you have checked completely all insurance this person may hold.

Once you have ascertained financial status and insurance available, you must examine the types of facilities available in the area where you wish to seek placement.

There are a variety of places in almost every community which offer care to the elderly going under the collective heading: nursing homes. It can be very confusing. We will list here the most common types:

1. Personal Care Home—these are licensed to accept four (4) or fewer patients who need custodial or intermediate (not skilled) nursing care. They are almost always in the operator's own home. These homes recently have come under a great deal of fire from licensing agencies and many are going out of business. They are occasionally run by registered nurses, but more often by licensed practical nurses.

Medicaid (not Medicare) will pay for care in these homes which have fulfilled licensure requirements, but many other insurances will not.

2. Extended Care Facilities—these are nursing homes which have successfully fulfilled certification requirements through federal and state inspections to receive Medicare/Medicaid funds for care of covered patients. Many insurances which cover nursing home care accept Medicare/Medicaid standards. A patient with Medicare or Medicaid benefits can *only* be covered in a facility which has passed their certification requirement.

These homes are often doubly certified for skilled care (those patients requiring professional services under constant supervision by a registered nurse) and intermediate care (those patients for which the home receives lesser Medicaid remuneration for less intense care which does not require the continual presence of a registered nurse).

3. Church Homes—these are homes which have often been in existence for many years. They are sponsored by a particular religious affiliation and are frequently among the most gracious, charmingly appointed facilities one could imagine. Until recently most church homes provided only basically domiciliary care with small infirmaries available for sudden illnesses and heavy reliance on local hospitals for more serious illnesses. With the advent of Medicare/Medicaid many of these homes are increasing their level of professional medical in-house abilities to become certified as extended care facilities. They often have long waiting lists, but it is always worthwhile to explore placement within them.

4. Ethnic Homes—these are similar in approach to church homes.

5. Proprietary versus Non-Profit Homes—all homes fall into one of these categories. As a general rule, church, ethnic, state, county, or philanthropic homes are nonprofit. Those homes that are part of a chain or advertise heavily are usually proprietary (profit-making).

They run the gamut of professional competence. Do not rely on statements regarding the altruistic nature of a home as evidence of its abilities.

You are going to want to choose a home that answers the professional needs for the particular patient, accepts his insurance (if any), and that the patient or his family can manage financially when insurance benefits cease. At the same time you will need to explore how physicians' services are handled at each home.

III. Medical Facts

Again, you cannot begin to look adequately for a nursing home without a clear medical determination from your physician. You will need to request from him a clear, no-holds-barred prognosis. At the same time ask him to spell out for you those areas in which he expects both improvement and problems.

You will need his evaluation as to whether he sees this nursing home placement as permanent, long-term, or short-term. You are not bound for all time by his findings, but they are an essential beginning point. Have your physician spell out for you exactly what special services and/or equipment will be necessary and what you should look for.

You will want to question: Is there a house physician? How are emergencies handled? How fast is emergency care available? Will the physician presently caring for the patient be able to continue care at this nursing home? Where is the nearest hospital?

These are all questions that any competent nursing home should be able to answer clearly and concisely.

IV. Social and Aesthetic Facts

The senior citizen entering a nursing home is, by this very act, giving up much of what he holds most precious. He is leaving his home, possessions, friends, and familiar surroundings.

It is very important that, if at all possible, you try to protect what you can of past habits, friends, and interests. Usually a person will prefer to stay in the geographic area where he has been living. If there is no other choice but to move the person to another area, then make the best of it by being supportive. If there is a choice, however, consider placement where friends, clubs, hobbies, familiar entertainment are all still available.

Older people often have difficulty getting around

and a centrally located home, where public transportation enables friends to stay in touch, is always desirable.

Take a careful look at this person's habits and preferences. Question closely all nursing homes you visit as to whether there will be any problems or restrictions in maintaining these.

What about church affiliation? If this is an important part of this person's life, will he still be able to participate? Or at the other extreme, is it mandatory?

What about restrictions placed by the home? Question administrators carefully regarding their policy of acceptance. For instance, some homes will not admit patients who are noisy. Many confused elderly do cry out in the night. If this is going to be a problem, discuss it carefully with the director of nursing and administrator before proceeding with an admission.

Spend some time considering day-to-day living. What things about the patient's past lifestyle will be important here? Is this a solitary person who enjoys being alone? A double room might be torture to such a person. Is this a person who derives much pleasure from radio, television, or records? Can these still be a part of his daily life? Will the home permit these things in his room?

Finances may dictate the choice of double or single room. If the patient is someone who has always enjoyed company and basically dislikes being alone, a double room may be the answer. (See Chapter 4 for a more complete breakdown of evaluating patient's needs and what one should watch for in various nursing homes.)

V. Actual Inspection

This is a crucial step and probably one of the most difficult for most families. If you are like the vast majority of people you've never seen a nursing home. Or you have have visited an old aunt or uncle in one years ago, and dimly remember it as a depressing situation you wanted to leave immediately. Try to forget these past impressions.

Many nursing homes today are bright, airy, cheerful institutions. The following guidelines are meant to help you look below surface impressions and do some fact-finding on your own.

After you have worked through the initial steps outlined in this chapter, you have probably come up with a list of 2–8 nursing homes that seem suitable. Now you must actually visit these institutions. Never admit anyone to a home unless you have gone through it *yourself*. You can never rely on word-of-mouth. It is notoriously bad!

Now then—set down on paper the names and addresses of those homes you have selected. Your first step is to phone each institution and ask for some general information.

1. *Is the home licensed?* By what agency? What is the date of the current license? Will it be available for you to see when you visit? Is the administrator licensed? When was their last inspection? Did they receive unrestricted licensure?

2. *Can you visit?* Can you see all areas of the home? To whom should you speak when you visit? If there is any hesitation or you find that all areas of the home cannot be visited, cross this home off the list immediately. Remember—the room the resident lives in is only one facet of a whole life. The food he eats comes from

a kitchen—probably served on a tray delivered by a cart. These should all be clean. The room where he/she showers or bathes is probably down another hallway—again, cleanliness and safety are necessary factors. The well-run home has nothing to hide and should be glad to show you all areas.

For a tour encompassing a whole home (especially a large one) we feel it is reasonable for the nursing home to ask you to come at a specific time so that a staff member can be free to escort you. However, you should *never* be turned away if you visit a home merely to observe general functioning on a patient floor. It is *not* your privilege to enter residents' rooms, as these are their homes and their rights should not be violated. It is your right to chat with anyone in hallways or public areas, and under no circumstances should this be stopped.

The best time to visit any home unannounced is during the evening meal hour. This is after most administrative staff have left for the day and staffing patterns are generally lower. Watch to see if residents are being fed promptly and kindly. Are there a lot of trays sitting around untouched? Do the aides seem busy? Do they seem cheerful or dour? Do the residents seem contented or unhappy? What is the noise level?

In general, if the staff is busy in a fairly calm way and seems to be interacting with residents, this is probably a pretty good situation. On the other hand, if you see clusters of staff members chatting with one another while trays sit around and residents appear discontented, this is probably not where you'd want your relative placed.

During a prearranged visit, you should expect to meet the administrator (or assistant) and the director of nursing (or assistant). They should be willing to show you the entire home, answer your questions, and explain anything you don't understand.

You should see the administrator's current license. (It should be hanging on a wall in his office with date readily readable.) You may ask to see the registered nurses' current licenses. Ask about professional coverage on a 24-hour basis. Any home certified as a skilled care facility is required by law to have a registered nurse on duty 24 hours a day.

Ask to see the home's current state license and/or Medicare/Medicaid certification. If any licenses are outdated, telephone the local Department of Human Resources and/or the Social Security office right after your visit and ask why.

All inspection records by state and federal officials are now considered matters of public record. These will be made available on request at your local Social Security office. They may be of limited value because they are often dated by the time they are filed and are sometimes hard to follow. If you have questions or doubts, though, they are another useful information source. (See "Certification," page 134.)

At the same time that you are touring the home, the staff should be asking you questions about the patient's present status and needs. Beware of the facility that promises you everything. Such promises are generally impossible to live up to. The home that admits it may not be able to provide for some needs is probably more thoughtfully run.

While you are walking through the home make use of all your senses to reach an opinion.

1. *Smell*—Is it generally pleasant? Do you smell urine or a close musty odor? Is there a strong smell of sweet room deodorants and a urine smell underneath? If so, you'd better think twice about this home. In any

home there will be occasional bad odors, but if the overall impression is odorous then something's wrong.

2. *Sight*—Is the appearance pleasant with a general impression of cleanliness? The floor may be buffed spotlessly, but are the corners full of dirt, and window sills and bureau and table tops dusty and spotted? Is the facility generally neat? Remember, people live here, so you must expect some articles of daily living to be lying around. Too neat can be as bad as dirty. If things are army neat one may wonder how much freedom residents actually have.

What is your general impression? Is it one of chaos or fairly good organization, allowing for a fair amount of activity? Look at the staff. Are their expressions generally pleasant? Do relationships with residents strike you as pleasant? Remember that many residents spend several years in nursing homes. In many good homes the personnel may seem too familiar with the patients. We generally regard this as a plus, not a minus. Often the elderly spend long periods of time without visits from family and friends. They have a great need to be touched and to feel needed and wanted. A staff member who is able to do this for a resident provides a great service.

Is the staff generally well dressed? By this we mean, do uniforms fit fairly well? Are their shoes falling apart? Is there a generally professional or purposely casual appearance? A staff that takes pride in its collective appearance usually feels pretty good about itself, its facility, and its residents, and shows it in the care given.

Be sure you see kitchens, bathrooms, dining areas. These should all appear clean and well cared for. Bathrooms must be large enough for wheelchair use.

There must be handrails beside toilet and tub. Privacy must be ensured by either doors or curtains.

Ask to be shown residents' rooms. These should also be clean, and neat. There should be some personal possessions around and generally a homelike atmosphere.

How do the residents look who are in the halls, public areas, or whom you glimpse in their rooms? Are they generally neat, combed, and comfortably dressed? Do you see evidence of some happiness or do they all appear apathetic, dejected, or agitated?

Keep in mind, however, that you are visiting a facility that is caring for many ill and infirm people. It would not be unreasonable to see someone with wet pants or a room that is disheveled or an agitated patient whom someone is trying to calm down. It is the overall impression that is important—not a single instance.

There should not be stacks of dirty linens either on floors of rooms or spilling out of hampers in utility rooms. Dirty laundry should be in large enough containers and emptied down laundry chutes or bagged and closed frequently.

3. *Hearing*—Be aware of the noise level and its quality. A good home will usually have a rather constant hum wth occasional outbursts and hopefully some laughter and conversation.

Does the staff talk with residents in a generally cheerful way? Remember that many patients are deaf and raised voices sometimes are essential. Angry voices are never essential, but there are times when a certain amount of firmness is necessary to handle a difficult resident.

4. *Touch*—Do surfaces feel clean? When residents

reach for your hand as you pass through a corridor (they *will* do this—don't be afraid, take their hands and stop a moment; you'll be performing a great kindness) are their hands clean, nails trimmed and well cared for? Are handrails (which should be present in all halls, elevators, bathrooms) clean, easy to grab? Do you feel sharp edges anywhere?

There are three areas not included in the above which are very important.

1. *Dining Areas*—If at all possible the home should have communal dining areas that are cheerful and pleasant where the majority of residents are encouraged to go. This form of socialization is very important and we give any home high marks that recognizes this.

2. *Safety*—This is an extremely important and difficult area to verify. You will do best here by going to your Social Security office and pulling the last inspection record and reading what the inspectors found.

In visiting homes you can ask to see several things to get a general impression of how careful they are:

a. Fire escapes and fire extinguishers (readily available on every floor?)
b. Fire drills (how often? written plan?)
c. Sprinkler system or fire doors?
d. Handrails in all areas and tight to walls?
e. Cleaning and other dangerous solutions marked and locked away?
f. Stairwells protected and marked so residents can't fall?

3. *Hidden costs* should be investigated thoroughly. This is very important, because in many homes the published room rental is only the beginning. Be sure to see in writing all other costs. These may include, but are not necessarily limited to

a. Hand feeding
b. Special diets
c. Laundry
d. Incontinent care (changing bedding, pants and/or diapers)
e. Drugs
f. Physician's visits
g. Supplies (catheters, special utensils)
h. Occupational, physical therapies

Many homes charge $1.50–$4.00 per day for items a–d. Items e–f can be much more, depending on residents' needs. Question the administrator and nursing director closely and accept no evasive answers.

FOUR

Preparations for Entry to a Nursing Home

Choosing the right nursing home is just the first of many steps the whole family has to take together to make the experience positive. Our purpose in this chapter is to show how to minimize the effects of institutionalization by thoughtful preparation of the resident and family prior to entry. If, as is stated in the book *A Life Apart,* institutionalization is seen by the resident as "rejection," then we must attempt to lessen the trauma and loss. Keep in mind that life for the elderly is a series of losses to which they adjust remarkably well. Nursing home placement will be viewed as yet another loss, perhaps one of the largest a person must face. Normally, we find and receive love in the company of close relatives and friends, those with whom we live. Entering a nursing home deprives one of this contact. We should ask what practical steps will ease the transition, and which of these steps can be planned ahead?

If you were accepting a new member into your family, probably on a permanent basis, what would you like to know about him? What preparations would you like to make? Would you like to know his habits? Would you find it helpful to know what he will bring and when it will arrive? The more a nursing home knows about a person in advance or immediately upon admission, the more comfortable the resident can be made to feel. Since a move to a nursing home is often made without much warning, as in Mrs. Jones' case, you may wonder how the topics described in this chapter can apply in such a situation. Pre-planning is the ideal method. But if events do not allow it, follow the suggestions here as soon after admission as possible.

In order to ensure the home's knowledge of the most important details about your relative or friend, we strongly suggest that you put in writing information covering the following items.

1. *Diet.* Does the resident eat well or must he be encouraged? Has the doctor ordered any past dietary restrictions? The physician may or may not include such information in a medical history. Does the resident try to sneak foods not included on the diet? For instance, we often find cookies in the clothes drawer of a diabetic resident. Another example is the cardiac patient on a low salt diet who always seems to have a cache of salted peanuts. Are there any religious dietary restrictions? What are the resident's particular likes and dislikes? While personal tastes cannot always be followed, some may be met. Older people often find that certain foods cause an uncomfortable amount of "gas." Specify these foods. Are there any food allergies? What time has the new resident been used to eating? If the timetable is very different, supplemental feedings may have to be given in order to adjust to a new schedule without discomfort. What time was the main meal of the day eaten? How many meals are eaten a day? Many elderly people like frequent small feedings.

2. *Mobility.* By mobility we mean the ability to get around. How active is this elderly person? The doctor who examines the resident prior to entry will undoubtedly indicate how mobile the person has been. In addi-

tion, he may indicate whether physical therapy will be of some help either in maintaining or increasing present mobility. For instance, an older person might be fairly steady at home and move around unaided. Indicate whether the older person will have some difficulty moving around in strange surroundings. Is his eyesight poor? Those with poor eyesight need the familiar placement of objects in order to feel secure. Has this person done any kind of special exercises? Note these habits so they can be followed through at the nursing home.

3. *Mental Status.* Many older people become confused in unfamiliar surroundings, especially at night. Do you notice this in your relative or friend? Does he know where he is, who he is, and what day of what year it is? For safety reasons this information is very important.

4. *Ability to Care for Self.* Has this elderly person been bathing himself prior to entry? Does he need some help or does he require complete care? What has been the pattern up until this time? Does he prefer a bath or a shower? Maybe the nursing home has only tubs and the resident has always showered. The nursing personnel would like to know this so they can explain such changes to the new resident before subjecting him to something new.

5. *Religion.* What church, if any, does the resident attend? Is religion important to the resident? Is there a particular minister or church member who will visit regularly? Will he attend church in the home?

6. *Are there other habits that would be helpful for the nursing home staff to know?* Does the resident smoke? Does he understand that he can only smoke in certain areas, and never in bed? Usually residents are not allowed matches so that the nursing staff will know who

is smoking where. This, of course, is for everyone's protection; however, it may also be quite an upsetting change for someone who is unprepared. Is alcohol part of the daily routine? Suppose the new resident has always had a glass of sherry before the evening meal. What a shock it would be to find on his first night in a nursing home that it is unavailable. Find out from the doctor whether he will write a prescription for it and be sure that the prescription is included with the admission papers. Bring the sherry with you and give it labelled to the person in charge. These small habits are important to observe. Their immediate availability gives a sense of continuity to both the resident and staff. We have seen residents who have always chewed tobacco or snuff. If a nurse saw a resident with dark brown saliva she would be very concerned unless she knew the resident was a tobacco chewer. All of these suggestions make good care and continuity easier for the nursing staff. At the same time the resident will obviously benefit. Give the staff, preferably the director of nurses, a copy of your summary and keep one yourself.

Having planned for the actual admission together, and having put your thoughts on specific personal habits in writing for the nursing staff, what further can you do in preparation? Personal belongings are a matter of great importance to someone moving away from familiar surroundings. You must find out what the resident wants to bring, what is allowed, and then itemize and label everything from nighties to radios.

When you are making arrangements for entry into a nursing home ask the administrator, social worker, or director of nurses what can be brought from home. Attitudes vary greatly, but thoughtful administrators will make every effort to meet personal needs. Is it permissible to bring favorite pictures and a mirror to hang on the wall? Some homes allow personal furniture, especially in an older building. Newer nursing homes often have built-in bureaus, bookcases, and desks. The older nursing homes may be more flexible. If Mrs. Jones, for instance, had always sat in a particular chair, she might have been able to bring this with her. A word of caution is advisable here. If you plan to take a favorite chair that is dirty, has vermin, or is wet from urinary incontinence, be sure it is fumigated and cleaned before bringing it into the home. We have seen cockroaches emerge from cherished chairs more than once. Curtains are usually not allowed unless they meet the fire safety standards. Ask the social worker or the administrator about this if you are planning to bring some. Bedspreads are usually acceptable; however, be sure they are washable unless you are prepared to take care of them yourself. Rugs are rarely allowed for safety reasons. Furniture and wheelchairs do not move easily over rugs. Residents may trip on them. In addition, they are difficult to clean. Lamps may be in order, especially a good reading lamp. Older persons need very good light directly on the page in order to use best what may be diminishing eyesight. Television, radio, a large numbered clock, and a calendar can be very consoling to a lonely person away from home. A hospital bed is usually provided, in case more intensive nursing care is needed. A bed which can be raised is easier for the nursing staff. A hospital bed would be more unusual in a personal care home, but normal in a skilled care home.

As we have mentioned in the chapter on choosing a nursing home, there are different methods of charging for goods and services. When you are helping to assemble the personal effects to go to the nursing home, ask about such items as facial tissue, soap, bath powder, toothbrush, and toothpaste. Sometimes these items are included in the basic price. A small shop for notions, run by residents or volunteers, may be located on the premises. However, it may be less expensive to take advantage of a sale at your local pharmacy or grocery. In any case, should you bring these items, we advise you to bring only a small supply at any one time. They have a way of being borrowed. Label these items with name and room number whenever possible.

Clothes should be numerous enough to meet whatever laundry schedule you decide upon. They should be designed to meet the particular physical needs of each elderly person. For instance, a resident who is incontinent and confined to a wheelchair, will need more clothes than someone who has control of both bowel and bladder and is up and around. Think carefully about this, and ask questions of either the social worker, nurse, or your doctor. What will be suitable clothing? Someone who is receiving simply custodial care should continue to wear his usual clothes. Remember, however, that not all fabrics survive commercial laundering. If the resident will be washing clothes himself either by hand or in a laundermat in the home, or if the clothes will be privately washed, then a fair amount of flexibility is possible. If, however, the nursing home laundry which washes linens will be used, the clothes must be sturdy and preferably made of cotton. Commercial laundry detergents are strong and the water is particularly hot.

For a female resident confined to a wheelchair, it is often more convenient for dresses and slips to be split up the back. This allows for easy dressing and undressing. Simply sew up any front opening and slit the garment down the back. Add ties or Velcro fasteners.

We have not found as simple an answer for men's clothes. Loose-fitting pants are easier to handle and more comfortable than tight-fitting ones; cotton or synthetic, please. Men's wool pants are a problem. Should the resident, male or female, be bedridden, nightgowns or pajamas split up the back are more convenient.

Undergarments should be purchased with the same general principles in mind. If a commerical laundry is used, be sure the garments are cotton or a washable synthetic. Ladies in wheelchairs will find garter belts easier to manage than girdles for holding up stockings. Although they are sometimes difficult to find, usually the less expensive stores will carry them. A tight garter around the knee should not be worn because the elastic will shut off the blood circulation in the leg. This can be both dangerous and uncomfortable. Pantyhose work well for some women. A lap robe for warmth and modesty is sometimes more easily managed by both men and women in place of or in addition to stockings or trousers.

Shoes can be very important. If an elderly person has any kind of specially built shoe be sure to bring it to the nursing home. Any shoe must be comfortable. A resident who walks should have supportive shoes for extra stability. The soles should not be slippery. For someone confined to a wheelchair a slipper is satisfactory. If the slipper is loose, add a tie or not too tight elastic over the arch to keep the slipper on. We often find slippers which have fallen off. One slipper will be found in the middle of the hall, unmissed.

Washable, loose-fitting sweaters for men and shawls or loose sweaters for the ladies are the easiest to use. If a resident is stiff with arthritis, a shawl is easier to manage. Bathrobes and dressing gowns should be washable and warm. Remember, a person who is sitting still requires warmer clothes than one who is moving about. A bathrobe is often worn to and from the bathroom, which may or may not be adjacent to the room.

If proper clothes and other necessities are not available to you, be sure that the social worker or administrator knows this. Often suitable donations are available. Volunteers sometimes collect clothing for the needy elderly. Outdoor clothing should be included unless the resident will be confined to bed.

Label everything that is brought into the nursing home, even shoes and socks. You can buy a permanent laundry marker at any drug or department store. Use it. Make a list of every item, large or small. This protects the resident and the nursing home. Give one copy to whomever admits the resident and keep one for yourself. Often an elderly person becomes temporarily confused on being admitted to a nursing home. He may not remember what was brought and what was left behind. A list gives you both something solid to refer to.

As placement preparations are being made, there are some issues which should be explored. These are sensitive and psychological. Talking about them will help the resident build some coping mechanisms. A list of these issues includes the following:

1. other residents
2. single or double room
3. valuables
4. personal hygiene
5. food
6. visiting
7. staffing

Minnie Jones, who was moved quickly and without preparation, was ill-prepared for daily life in the nursing home. I doubt that her children had any notion of what it would be like. If they had known, they were too rushed to tell Minnie. They purposely planned to spare her any details. However, these issues are real and traumatic. If they cannot be "talked out" prior to admission there should be opportunity for discussion after.

In the second chapter, we discussed general information about residents of the nation's nursing homes. We know these people are primarily female, about 80 years old, and have one or more chronic debilitating conditions. What does this really mean? One must be realistic about the kinds of people who will be in the institution. Visiting various nursing homes you were undoubtedly repulsed, shocked, and made uncomfortable by the people you saw. Now think of your friend or relative who is going to live in such a home. How are you going to prepare her? Again, you must be comfortable yourself with the situation before you can impart a measure of support to another. Think how Mrs. Jones must have looked physically when entering the nursing home. She was frail, pale, and in a wheelchair. Physical shock and psychological trauma may have made her eyes appear lifeless. She may not have been very rational. Her fingers could have been bent and contorted from arthritis. She may have had a tremor. Now imagine a nursing home full of Mrs. Joneses, some slightly worse, some somewhat better in appearance. This scene is what shocked you at first. You are viewing the normal aging process plus the ravages of chronic disease in concentrated form. Minnie, actually, had a definite personality with strengths and weaknesses. Become acquainted with these people who will be your relative's co-residents, for each can share a wealth of experience which will quickly make you forget outward appearances. We also urge that any children who can be comfortable with the elderly should be encouraged to visit them. Both young and old will benefit substantially from such visits. If Mrs. Jones had been in better health and had needed only custodial care, she might have become very depressed by the nursing home, since she was not adequately prepared. None of us likes to be reminded of the discomforts that may await us as we age.

Financial considerations may determine whether a resident will occupy a single or double room. On the other hand, the home may offer only singles or doubles. In some homes three or four must share a room. If the patient would prefer solitude, but finances allow for only a double room, then the only thing to do is make the best of it. Be sure to see the room and meet the roommate. Look realistically at the situation. Are these two people likely to be able to live together or do you see obvious problems? For instance, you might be visiting and note that your friend's roommate is moderately deaf; speaks loudly, is gregarious; likes to watch TV all day; wants the windows open and the room cool with the shades up. You know that your relative is a quiet contemplative type who reads voraciously and finds TV a hateful distraction. Since cataract surgery two years ago bright sunlight is uncomfortable to his eyes. He has always liked drawn curtains and an overly warm environment. The adjustment potential for these two people is poor from the start. They should not be forced together if any alternative is available. Explore all the possibilities with the nursing director and administrator. They usually come up with answers, since their best interests involve keeping residents as content as possible.

Another consideration is the room's nearness to the nurses' station. While rounds are made and all residents checked frequently by the staff, those nearer the central station can more easily call out if they require attention. This is usually an advantage if the patient is very ill, badly disabled (so that if the call bell is out of reach he is virtually incommunicado), or comatose. Should the resident be confused and easily frightened, the activity around the nurses' station is comforting. The drawback to this area is that it is usually the noisiest spot on the floor. At shift changes or during problem times the activity and discussion can be disconcerting. Many alert and semi-independent residents prefer being further removed from this area.

Death is a reality in nursing homes. It is not always anticipated and you must face the fact that your loved one may have to live through the loss of several roommates. This is always traumatic, particularly when the residents have been friends. We have found, though, that often the elderly handle this much better than the young. In general, they are able to be fairly fatalistic, particularly if the staff has been kind and supportive.

In addition to the personality differences involved between roommates there are other issues which revolve around life in a room with someone else. How can privacy be maintained? In preparing your relative discuss the fact that there are curtains or screens between the beds, assuming they exist. If they are not in evidence, demand such a partition. Decide together, if personal furniture can be brought to the home, how each piece would fit into the total room as well as what would best suit your relative's immediate needs.

At this juncture let us discuss the situation of the husband and wife who will be entering the nursing home together. If they have lived together and slept in the same room for many years, be sure to try to find a home that will allow them to continue this way. Innumerable times we have heard relatives say, "Mom and Dad always fight, so we thought they should have separate rooms," or, worse yet, suggest that they be in separate homes. Who are we to judge a long relationship? It is their life and it must be their decision and no one else's. If they enjoy bickering, let them. We have always sensed that a little stress probably keeps them functioning! If a room together is impossible then be sure they have rooms as close as possible and allow them time alone behind closed doors. They have needs, too, both emotional and sexual, and you must be sure that their privacy will be respected.

Possessions give a person a sense of pride, security, and identity. A gold watch with a personal inscription, received upon retirement, could be a conversation piece. A woman might find solace in a locket her mother had given her. Suppose it is a valuable antique or a piece of jewelry which gives an elderly person great comfort. Can this be safely taken with her to the nursing home? Should it be put into storage or a bank vault? Is it worth the risk of loss to have it with her? This is an emotional subject, but you would do well to iron out a decision before entering. Suppose Mrs. Jones had a valuable engagement ring which she usually removed at night before retiring. This might well disappear for reasons discussed in Chapter 7. She should be advised to keep it on or put it in the nursing home safe. Without adequate preparation this situation can make a person feel very stripped and angered.

Bathroom and bathing facilities and procedures are

other essential areas for discussion. The question of personal hygiene and toileting is often one of the most emotional and can leave a resident feeling completely defeated and utterly helpless. You will want to know the placement of the bathroom in relation to the resident's room. Can he walk to the bathroom? Are bedside commodes used in this home? How well is the resident's privacy protected if they are used? Are there shower or tub facilities or both? After making some inquiries of the director of nurses be prepared to be frank about the kinds of personal care which will be given. If an elderly person is no longer able to keep himself clean, the fact that a nurse or nursing assistant will perform these services for him should be discussed. If the patient has been in a hospital he may have experienced complete hygienic dependency. If, however, the resident is entering from his own home and is unable to care for himself, he should be prepared for a nurse or orderly to accompany him to the bathroom. Imagine yourself in completely new surroundings with a total stranger lifting you into the bathtub and bathing you. Modesty should be preserved with bath blankets and towels; however, even with these precautions the experience can be shattering. On the positive side, of course, is the fact that the elderly person will feel much fresher, and this should be stressed.

Food is so very important to anyone confined to a nursing home that it deserves special consideration. The quality of the food will vary from good to bad; however, it will never equal home cooking. On the positive side, though, mealtimes in a central dining room may be a welcome change for an older person who has been living and eating alone. Mrs. Jones may have found it very difficult to be enthusiastic about cooking for herself and then eating alone after so many happy years of social meals. She probably would have benefited from more regular meals and someone with whom to eat. In preparing to discuss mealtimes in a nursing home, you should obtain a menu plan from the administrator of the home. Will there be a choice of foods? Are there any favorite dishes included on the menu? Is it possible for you to bring special foods to the resident? Build bridges between home and nursing home whenever possible.

Visiting should be a positive force in the transition, and the elderly resident should have some say in planning. Urge the resident to invite you over at his convenience and discuss how often your schedule will permit a visit. Leave the resident as much control over his life as possible by giving him some input into the visiting plan. In addition, assure him that your concern and love will remain even during his confinement.

One last subject which you should consider is that of the staff. We have included in Chapter 7 a lengthy discussion of how to approach the staff to the mutual benefit of the resident, the staff, and the family. You should, however, lay the groundwork for a good relationship prior to admission. The most difficult area to face is prejudice. It is never pretty but it exists and must be met head-on. The elderly sometimes have had experiences which have fixed their views of minorities. Many have had no opportunity for contacts which would have caused attitudes to change. Those people performing the most intimate tasks in nursing homes are often from minority groups. It happens frequently that the resident suddenly finds himself in the untenable position of being forced to deal with people whom he has always distrusted and perhaps feared, no matter how misguided the feeling. He will lash out with anger and often verbal cruelty. The staff know this well and for the most part handle the situation with understanding. It is, however, potentially explosive and problems do arise.

If you know or think that your relative or friend feels this way about those who will be caring for him, it is essential that this be dealt with openly and honestly with the nursing home personnel, and with the resident. This will not magically erase all bad feelings but it will open communication and allow people to express their emotions in healthier directions.

Some miscellaneous items which should be attended to before admission are the following:

(1) Usually a physical exam is required prior to entry. This must be completed by a licensed physician. A chest x-ray may be necessary. Be sure to know how medical care will be provided: your own physician or a house doctor, etc.

(2) Make sure you understand all financial arrangements and do not sign any contract unless it is clear to you. You may always ask to take a copy with you to get an independent judgment from a lawyer. Do this before you sign something you do not understand.

(3) Be sure you understand your responsibilities as well as those of the nursing home. A nursing home is not a substitute for the family and friends. The burden is still primarily upon YOU.

(4) Many nursing homes will require you to make funeral arrngements before entry. We recommend that this be done long before the emotional trauma of death occurs even if it is not required by the nursing home.

In conclusion, aspects of planning which ideally come before admission can be taken care of afterwards as time permits. However, do not use that as an excuse for avoiding the issues. Many of the facts stressed here will be discussed in further detail in later chapters. Lastly, may we suggest some rules of thumb for any discussions between family, friends, and resident:

—Be realistic in talking with the elderly about what to expect in a nursing home. Raise expectations only when they can be met. For instance, it would be cruel to decide between you that you would visit once a day and then come only once a week.

—Leave hope for the future within the limits of possibility. Is there hope, for instance, that daily physical therapy could improve stability to enable walking with assistance?

—Keep communication open, for that is the key to success. There was precious little communication, despite the good intentions, in the case of Minnie Jones. Her story shows what trauma such a course of action can bring to everyone concerned.

FIVE

Reactions to Placement

"Because institutional living is not the typical living arrangement for people in our society, the impact on the individual who enters an institution or other congregate facility can be traumatic in the extreme." [1]

Dr. Kastenbaum makes three further pertinent points in discussing the effect of institutionalization. First, the loss of significant people and familiar objects can be devastating, producing a feeling of defeat and uselessness. Second, the security of well-learned patterns of daily living and environmental clues is suddenly swept away. Third, "The newly-institutionalized elderly person becomes anchorless, often rejected and unloved; rudderless, without family or familiar guidelines. In a milieu quite foreign to his experiences he frequently adapts by bizarre defensive behavior that further isolates him from his fellows." [2]

Minnie Jones suddenly found herself residing in a nursing home before she realized what was happening. It is not surprising that she reacted with petulant behavior and anger. Over and over we have witnessed the trauma that occurs when an adult finds himself stripped of decision-making powers and essentially tricked into admission.

This is always a difficult emotional time. It can be made easier if several key words are kept in mind. These are:

1. Honesty
2. Time
3. Conversation
4. Dignity
5. Patience

This chapter will be devoted to explaining what we mean by these words in this context and discussing why people have similar reactions to placement.

Honesty

We have stressed repeatedly the value of *honest* discussion about nursing home placement with the resident. This policy must be continued during and after admission. Once a person actually enters a nursing home many of the same questions which have been discussed before admission may be asked. The shock of placement may make the resident question once again why he or she needs to be there. You may verbally have to go through the entire placement process once again to reassure the resident that he does belong there. This process may go on for weeks.

It is indeed true that total honesty can be initially difficult. Stubbornness and angry hurt are very real emotional problems. Keep in mind, however, that if you don't confront these problems before admission they will be doubly difficult to handle after the move has been made. Tact and understanding will be necessary. Real physical problems may prevent a return home. The initial explanation may not suffice. It will have to be repeated, and as often as necessary. This can be difficult and trying. We firmly feel that if such a dramatic change has to be made in this person's life it is only fair that the reasons for this be honestly expressed to him. As previously stated this holds true even if the person is confused or comatose. Be sure to explain the situation completely. You have no way of knowing how much information a comatose person absorbs. It is our belief that more information is assimilated than we might imagine.

Time

Admission to a nursing home is a time-consuming process. The whole procedure will go more smoothly if on the day the move is to be made you are entirely free of other obligations. Devote the entire day to it. Most nursing homes require or request that admissions take place about midmorning. A new resident should enter a home at peak staffing time. Mid-morning admission allows time for some settling-in before evening. There are a myriad of details, all of which will take more time than expected, associated with the admission procedure. These run the gamut of unpacking, signing forms, showing the new resident around, and meeting staff members. The placement of phone, TV, and radio in the room will also take time. We have advised that the customs and requirements of the home be ascertained before admission. Spend time on this day familiarizing the new resident with these. For example, meal hours in most homes are pre-set. In order to handle the logistics of feeding a large number of people those hours must be strictly adhered to. If the new resident has been used to eating dinner about 7 or 8 P.M. and the dinner hour at this home is 5 P.M. she is likely to react with displeasure to the earlier time. As a practical matter you are not going to be able to change the established dinner hour. It may take several days for her to be comfortable with this schedule. Make an effort to have her accept the meal. Tell her to eat only what she wants initially. If necessary, arrange with the staff for a slightly heavier midevening snack for a few days. *The goal is to have things as comfortable and familiar as possible while adapting to some of the institutional requirements.*

The time requirement continues after admission day. When someone you care for enters a nursing home he needs your continuing support and this often involves many hours. A person will soon cease to care about himself if he feels that those about him have abandoned him. It is imperative that you continue to visit at frequent intervals. Remember, you and other family and friends are this person's link with the outside world. The more interested, caring, and supportive you are, the better will be his adjustment to the home.

Time is also a factor in trips outside the home. Whenever it is possible the nursing home resident should be invited out of the home to participate in holiday and family festivities. If the resident is truly unable to attend, take the festivities to the home or the bedside. Be sure that the resident has a part in the decisions regarding any such occasion.

Conversation

All human beings thrive and grow on meaningful conversational exchange. When senior citizens enter a nursing home they usually feel cut adrift from the mainstream of life. They feel powerless in the institutional environment. The resident, initially, may have difficulty communicating on any indepth basis with nursing home personnel. You, family members, and friends need to stand ready both to listen and initiate discussion. The newly admitted resident is often unable to communicate his feelings. He needs you to take the lead. You can help in a variety of both abstract and practical ways. Help him to find out whom to talk with about procedural difficulties within the home. To whom should he go with problems? Help him identify the questions he wants to ask and the things he wants to know. Don't be afraid to ask how he's feeling about his situation. When the resident wants to discuss something which makes you uncomfortable, *don't run from it.* There may be tears. Don't try to turn these off. Be supportive and willing to listen. He needs to talk this out.

A resident, in order to get along in the nursing home, may save all the complaints for the family or close friends when they visit. Everyone has stresses and strains in daily life and the elderly person in a nursing home is no exception. There are many ways of coping with these frustrations: exercising, talking with a confidant, or becoming engrossed in a project. These avenues and others may not be available to the nursing home resident; therefore, complaining to the family and close friends becomes the only recourse. Your job then is to *listen.*

How do you turn the tide, after the complaints are aired? It is very easy to become mired in these troubles. Some time must be spent on more positive subjects for the emotional health of the resident and the family. Who wants to come back for a visit where the only subjects of conversation are complaints? Some practical suggestions are:

(1) Bring a photo album of the family as a source of topics for discussion.
(2) Save some decision in relation to your life about which you could seek the residents advice: i.e., what to wear? What color trim to put on a dress, etc.
(3) Write some letters together to favorite people.

(4) Get a favorite book and read together.

(5) Travel magazines for a traveler can be a great source of entertainment. You will learn something as you look at them together.

(6) Make a family tree together. There will be lots of anecdotes you may be glad you heard.

(7) Arrange to visit another resident and talk or play a game together.

While we're on the subject of talk there is another phenomenon which occurs especially when a person has just been admitted to a home. The family may suddenly hear rather horrible tales about the nursing home personnel and what they are doing to the resident. You must take each complaint offered by your relative and search carefully for the source. Occasionally, real abuses do take place in a home and must be severely dealt with by proper authorities. More often the truth falls into a gray or middle area. The new resident is giving up familiar possessions and surroundings. He is abandoning lifelong habits and styles, trading them for a scheduled existence. At the same time total strangers are suddenly participating in the most intimate aspects of his day-to-day living. These strangers are often people of completely different lifestyles, customs, and sometimes language. It is little wonder that there are misunderstandings. You, as the mediator, have the difficult task of sorting all these out. Our advice is to look at each instance objectively. Enlist the help of the nursing supervisors and administrator if necessary. Where you do find innocent answers to problems, carefully explain to the resident exactly what happened. At the same time, if the new resident has unusual habits and personal styles, share these with the nursing home staff. They are often more than willing to go along with these idiosyncrasies. They appreciate having this information which they might not discover independently, or might learn only after a number of months.

Many times people dislike going to visit relatives in nursing homes because they literally don't know what to say. The truth is that scintillating conversation is unnecessary. You can utilize some of the techniques mentioned earlier and conversation can actually be minimal. The resident will derive as much enjoyment from your physical presence as from the spoken word. Remember also that those things he most often wants to hear are those things you consider most mundane. It is the everyday homely facts that make him feel he is still an active family participant.

Dignity

The person who has suddenly given up much of what has always been important to him stands in real danger of losing his own sense of dignity and self-worth. He needs to draw heavily on those around him to maintain and regain a sense of self. He finds himself in a dependent position. It is fairly easy to abandon pride and independence. He may become demanding in a demeaning way. Family and friends play an essential role here. The first thing to protect fiercely is his importance. You must seek and point out to him all the ways that he is important to those around him. These truths may have to be reinforced daily. Enlist his assistance and help in as many ways as possible. Ask his opinion about decisions to be made. Include him in family discussions and fill him in on current events. An elderly person has probably lived through a variety of problems in his own life. He will quickly sense problems in those he cares for. There is nothing wrong with discussing family difficulties. He will appreciate having been consulted and can often add good practical advice.

Dignity goes hand in hand with personal appearance. You must reinforce this person's pride. Be sure that basic grooming tools are readily available. If this person is so handicapped that he cannot groom himself be sure it is done for him. Nursing home staff members should be expected to follow through on cleanliness, hair combing, and tooth brushing. The resident should be in clean clothing. If the resident is confused the nursing assistants may choose the daily clothing and hair style. This may not be the style you personally would choose, but it is not appropriate for you to be angry with the staff for not knowing this. You do have a right and an obligation to complain if you find the resident's dignity compromised by decreased staff attention to basic cleanliness or to embarrassing exposures.

Family and friends have a responsibility to see that the resident is adequately supplied with brushes, deodorant, underwear, appropriate clothing, sweaters, nightwear, stockings, and well-fitting shoes or slippers. We have witnessed examples of residents with only one or two poorly repaired items of apparel and relatives who could never understand why the residents looked in such disarray.

Patience

You will be expected to draw on all of your reserves of understanding during the initial phase of nursing home admission. Patience is essential. You will see your loved one in a situation foreign to both of you. You may witness behavior and reactions in him that you simply cannot imagine.

The first day or so after a person has moved into a nursing home is usually a quiet time. It takes time to realize that one has actually given up a whole way of life and possibly will spend the rest of one's life in an institutional setting. It is almost always true that within a few days to weeks after admission a resident will react to the situation with anger and despair. This reaction can take many forms.

Confused or senile people often respond with agitated behavior and may actually attempt to leave. They often decide they're in a hotel and express a reasonable wish to return home. They are understandably distressed when they are stopped by staff members. These residents should have as many of their possessions as possible at hand and relatives should stay in close contact.

It is true that sometimes visits from relatives will increase this initial agitation. The desire to return home is reawakened each time a visit takes place. Occasionally in difficult situations the home will ask that relatives not visit for a few days while the new resident is becoming familiar with his new life. If you do elect to follow this course be sure to have frequent phone contact with the home and visit again as soon as possible.

Comatose patients also react to admission. They become increasingly restless and occasional stomach or bowel upsets (probably from changes in food) occur.

The majority (like Minnie Jones) react to placement in a slower, more difficult way. To give up so many things at once is a great blow. The new resident feels a natural need to be in control of himself and his environment. As he realizes that many things are now outside his control panic often ensues. He lashes out at all around him. Anger takes many forms. Minnie Jones was typical. Since it was the nursing assistants with whom she had most contact, and who were also performing the most intimate tasks for her, she feared and resented them most. They represented all she had lost. She was unable, at that point, to realize that they had nothing much to do with her present situation. Her feelings of helplessness and frustration made her actually hate these men and women.

Another typical reaction is to become angry at family members. A senior citizen is admitted to a home and angrily decides that his son or daughter just wants to be rid of him and steal everything he has. To be sure, this does happen sometimes, but we have seen many instances where such accusations are simply not true. The family in this situation has no choice but to remain supportive and not turn against the resident, no matter how vituperative he or she may be. It is distressing and difficult but stick with it. Your relative will adjust more quickly if loving care is not withdrawn at a crucial moment. Don't hesitate to involve the nursing supervisor or director in your problem. They can provide support and maybe some practical suggestions for helping to calm things down.

Depression and fear underlie all of these reactions. Severe depression in the form of withdrawal, loss of appetite, and lethargy is a very real and significant problem in some nursing home admissions. Some residents completely give up. Sometimes a resident will die within a very short time after admission. This is a problem that needs the concentrated attention of family, physician, nurses, clergy, and everyone who cares about this individual. In short, nursing home admission is always a difficult situation for both family and resident. However, with increased attention to the five areas listed above we feel the process can be less traumatic.

Finally, we will discuss the extraordinary needs of people who have one of two kinds of handicaps. The blind and the deaf face special difficulties when taken out of familiar surroundings. Readaptation to a new environment is especially traumatic to those with sensory deprivation.

Blindness

A person who is blind can often do fairly well in comfortable familiar surroundings. A new environment can cause disorientation. He or she may appear mentally confused.

One must be specifically honest about what the home is like. The resident must be asked what things he must have within hand's reach. There may be items he cannot have or long-standing customs he will not be able to observe. Carefully explain this and plan together.

Time and conversation go hand in hand. On the day of admission you will need to walk the resident carefully around all areas of the home. Guide his hands to surfaces and explain carefully what each thing is. Show him where his call bell is located and have him practice using it several times. Walk him to his doorway and around the hallway. Place his hands on guide rails in halls and bathrooms. Walk him to the nurses' station and back again to his room several times. While you are doing all this introduce your relative to those staff members and residents you meet. Be sure that staff members are well aware that he is blind. Share with them any information on day-to-day living habits that may make adjustment easier.

A telephone, radio, or talking books are all things that can make a blind person feel less cut adrift. They will also help in maintaining his orientation to reality.

Deafness

The profoundly deaf person has usually made certain adjustments to living in his home environment. On admission to the nursing home he faces some real difficulties.

If this person relies on a hearing aid be sure it is in good working order on the day of admission and that there are spare batteries with it. Both the resident and nursing home staff need to know where the hearing aid will be kept when not in use.

Show the staff how to care for and maintain the appliance. Be sure the staff are well aware of this handicap. If the resident uses other means of communication such as reading lips or expecting written communications, tell the staff. Tell them also if the resident is unable to answer an intercom or telephone.

Non-verbal clues are essential to a deaf person. You, as a familiar person, will be very important in the adjustment period. You will be the stabilizing influence while the deaf resident builds auxiliary lines of communication in his new home.

Just as a resident undergoes certain emotional reactions and adjustments upon entering a nursing home, so do family and friends. The reaction will vary in intensity depending upon the depth of the relationship prior to separation. These emotions may include any of the following: grief, anger, guilt, relief, or loss.

Let us return to Minnie Jones' family. We have not examined their emotional reaction to the placement of their mother in a nursing home. We said they were bewildered. Did they also feel guilty, angry, relieved, or all of these?

All three children must have felt some sense of guilt at having decided to have Minnie admitted to a nursing home. It is a normal reaction. They must have questioned whether they had really explored all the possibilities. We know that they made a reasonable decision. Guilt should have surrounded their lack of communication with Minnie. But Minnie's children had no knowledge of how to approach this crisis situation. Their mistake was a human one made out of love and concern. There is no way of changing the facts. Guilt may be real or unfounded. In either situation, the feelings must be explored in order to achieve some resolution and comfort. The children could have talked among themselves or with a third party such as a nurse, minister, or friend.

Minnie's family may have felt angry. They may have felt angry at Minnie for putting them in the position of having to place her in the home. They may have been angry at the staff for giving care in a way which was different from what they expected. They may have been angry at the nursing home for assuming control over their mother. These are natural feelings. Recognizing this eases the burden imposed by them.

Minnie's children may have felt relieved that their mother was safely placed in an appropriate home. A sense of relief is normal. If Minnie had been living at the home of one of her children, the sense of relief might have been even greater. When a family gears their life toward the care of one member in distress relief results when the responsibility is finally shared. An acute sense of loss may follow the initial relief. If life has been arranged around the needs of one person and suddenly that focal point is gone, the loss can be dramatic. It takes time to reorient life toward new goals and routines.

It is tragic that Minnie's family could not share their feelings of guilt, anger, and loss with her. The whole family would have benefited. Mrs. Jones knew how to cope with loss and could have comforted her children. She, in turn, would have felt useful and worthwhile. What can we learn from the experience of Minnie and her family? Grieving is a healthy and normal reaction to separation or death. Placement of a family member or friend in a nursing home often begins this process. Grief may incorporate all the reactions and emotions we have discussed. What is important to realize is that these emotional responses are expected. In accepting these facts, be sure you have someone with whom you can talk about your feelings: family, friend, clergy, nurse, social worker, or any interested person.

SIX

The Legal Status
of the Nursing Home Resident*

This chapter examines the common legal problems that accompany admission to a skilled nursing or intermediate care facility, particularly the rights, obligations, and remedies of nursing home residents in their dealings with the facility and staff which has undertaken their care. It will not attempt to resolve any specific legal problem. For any specific problem, one should see a competent attorney. Nevertheless, we hope that a clearer understanding of the legal status of the nursing home resident will contribute to a successful relationship with the facility providing the care. We shall present a general discussion of the following legal problems:

(a) The management and protection of the property and income of the nursing home resident and the selection of an attorney to help with this problem;
(b) Nursing home contracts;
(c) Patient's rights;
(d) The standards applicable to the institution and the care it must provide;
(e) The relationship between the nursing home resident and his or her doctor;
(f) Wills and "living wills."

* This chapter contributed by Joseph J. D'Erasmo, attorney, member of the bar, Maryland and New Jersey.

Pre-entry Planning and Nursing Home Contracts

This book is based on the premise that knowledge and planning in advance of an admission to a skilled nursing or intermediate care facility can prevent problems after admission. Common legal difficulties can also be avoided by careful advance planning.

One of the principal problems that accompanies a person to a nursing home is that of managing and preserving income and property. Even if the resident's only income is a social security check, managing those funds can present a problem. Frequently the prospective nursing home resident is unable, physically or mentally, to continue the routine economic tasks. Who is to help him with them or act for him? How can it be done "officially" and what protection is available against the possible misconduct of the person assisting the resident?

People are ingenious in devising unsuitable methods to resolve these issues. Joint accounts are opened with ambiguous, verbal expressions of intent regarding the true ownership and purpose of the joint account; powers of attorney are purchased at stationery stores and are completed by filling in the blanks; a trusted relative is naively expected to deal with the resident constantly, handling daily decisions regarding the resident's assets and expenditures. Wills are drawn by a family member or by the resident, or by a relative's attorney who has never represented the resident before; not uncommonly, no will is drawn because of reluctance to discuss the subject. And, unfortunately, there are occasional instances of people who seek to gain by taking advantage of an ailing nursing home resident.

As a result, the legal system has evolved a series of simple techniques to avoid or at least minimize these problems. Some of these methods are well known but they need to be emphasized here. Speaking realistically, the choice of solution and its implementation calls for the assistance of an attorney. If the nursing home resident or the family doesn't have a lawyer, how do you find one?

First, do not assume that the techniques mentioned below will require a great deal of legal expense, or that they are applicable only to those people with large personal estates. There are local attorneys who are well equipped to assist the average family with its routine legal problems, for fees within the family's means, just as there are physicians in family practice. If the situation requires the services of an attorney who specializes in a given type of problem, the attorney in general practice can help you find the specialist. Fees will vary, of course, depending on the nature of the problem, and the amount of time and skill required. There are legal aid programs to assist those people who qualify financially.

Use the following resources to find an attorney:

(1) The Martindale-Hubbell Legal Directory. This is a set of volumes found in most public libraries that lists lawyers by city and state. It tells you their age, their educational background, their prior employment experience, the number of years in practice, their specialties, and the way other lawyers and judges in the locality rate them as to legal ability and integrity. The directory does not rate every lawyer, so if the lawyer you have in mind has not been rated, don't draw any conclusions from that.

(2) Call the bar association of the county or city in which you live and ask their assistance in finding a lawyer. They will usually give you more than one reference (three is a magic number for some reason). Many

bar associations have a lawyer referral service, and they can also tell you about whatever public legal assistance plans are available.

(3) Ask your friends and neighbors about lawyers who have helped them with a similar problem, and double check their suggestions in Martindale-Hubbell.

When you've selected a particular lawyer, ask him what his consultation fee is for an initial one hour appointment. At that appointment you can get acquainted with the lawyer, get some ideas, and discuss the cost of doing what needs to be done.

There are many alternatives available to help you or your friend or relative manage income and property in a flexible but business-like manner.

For example, if the prospective patient is lucid and alert but physically disabled, a simple trust can be drawn revocable at his or her election, naming a trusted friend, a family member, or a banking institution as trustee. The trustee's obligations should be defined in the instrument. The property may be transferred to the trustee to be used for the care and protection of the resident. Upon the resident's death it will be distributed as the trust instrument directs. The instrument will also define the compensation of the trustee and will provide for a regular accounting to the resident or anyone designated by the resident to receive the account. The trust may be revoked at any time and the courts are always available if the trustee is incompetent or mercenary.

If the prospective resident is mentally incompetent and unable to designate a trustee, the court may appoint a guardian or conservator having jurisdiction to carry on essentially the same functions as a trustee. The guardian may be someone selected by the family, or by the court in the event of a dispute, and he or she must account to the court for the estate in his or her care.

Both of these methods are routine and simple devices for relieving, or assisting and protecting, the resident in managing his property and income at a time in life when physical or mental disability hinders him. Either method can be accomplished *before* entry into a nursing home, and it should be emphasized that neither method requires or presupposes the lunacy or incompetency of the resident. A guardian may be appointed for an incompetent, but it doesn't follow that the nursing home resident must be incompetent to employ a trustee or to have a guardian appointed.

The method of appointment is not difficult. In the case of a trustee it may be simply accomplished by the drafting of a document naming him, describing the assets and income to be transferred, and defining his obligations, compensation, and duty to account. No court order is necessary.

The appointment of a guardian does not involve much more, but usually a petition must be filed in the local court requesting the guardian's appointment and the court will then make the appointment.

A word of caution is needed about the use of joint accounts and powers of attorney. These devices should never be employed without professional advice. They may wind up creating more problems than they were intended to solve. It is true, for example, that a general power of attorney may be used as evidence of the authority of the holder to act for the person who granted the power, but in most states the power is automatically revoked by the incompetency, or death of the person who granted it.[1] Imagine the legal problems that could arise in a transaction occurring during or after such an event.

The trouble with joint bank accounts and other transfers of property, jointly, to the original owner and someone else is their ambiguity. That is, in the event of a dispute or a tax inquiry, a court may have to determine what the original owner intended: to transfer an actual ownership interest to the appointed joint owner, or to transfer the account or property in name only, as a convenience to the original owner in conducting his banking or the management of his real estate.

It is beyond the scope of this chapter to discuss the legal aspects of estate planning, including the tax consequences of trusts, guardianships, the joint ownership of property, and similar methods of preserving and developing the property and income of a prospective nursing home resident. The point is, see a lawyer *before* you sign in. Further, do not suppose that your relative must be wealthy to need or use these methods or to consult an attorney. Anybody with a modicum of property or regular income will benefit from the peace of mind afforded by planning and consultation with an attorney (privately retained or publicly provided) in advance of admission.

It is also in the period before admission that one of the most frequent (judging from the case law) sources of difficulty between the nursing home resident and the facility can be dealt with; that is, the problem of the so-called "life-care contract." This is an agreement proposed by many nursing home facilities whereby the resident turns over all of his or her assets to the facility in exchange for the facility's promise to care for the patient for the balance of his lifetime. Usually the contract contains a probationary period of six months or a year before it becomes effective.

Such contracts are lawful and they have been upheld many times by the courts against various kinds of legal challenges.[2] But they can lead to controversy and litigation if they are not properly understood and evaluated in advance. Before rejecting or accepting such a proposal, consider the obvious: what is the probable value, present and future, of the assets the resident is transferring to the institution, and what is the value, present and future, of the care-package the resident is getting in return? Viewed from this perspective an intelligent decision can then be made about that kind of contract. Certainly such a decision involves estimates of life expectancy, and accurate appraisals of the present and future value of existing assets. If you need expert help in making these decisions, get it before you or your relative sign the contract. Be aware, also, that assets acquired by the resident after he or she has signed such a contract and been admitted may be included in the contract.

What has been said above about life-care contracts is also applicable generally to any kind of agreement with a facility. If the facility doesn't routinely define its obligations to the resident in written form, ask the administrator for a letter which spells out the facility's obligations, its charges, and the resident's obligations. Request copies of its policies and regulations and read them, considering their effect on you or your relative. They could turn out to be more revealing than you might think. Ask for a detailed statement of the facility's promises to the resident and a list of what charges he or she will incur. This kind of information should be readily available.

Further, you should realize that if a family member or a friend signs the agreement with the facility, he or she may be assuming responsibility along with the resident for the charges to be incurred.

In short, do the obvious. Request a copy of any con-

tract in advance of admission, and read it before signing. It will mean what it says. If you don't understand
it, take it to a lawyer and ask him to review it with you
at his hourly rate. The investment will usually be well
worth it. Do not be afraid to request a modification of a
contract's terms or conditions. The institution may or
may not agree to a change, but at the very least you will
know more accurately what their actual position will
be, and you can react accordingly.

Patient's Rights

Perhaps the most important recent definition of standards for physical plant, personnel, management, and
all essential services that must be met by skilled nursing
and intermediate care facilities is contained in a
lengthy set of regulations which are part of the Federal
Medicare Health Insurance Programs for the Aged,
under the Social Security Act.[3] Any institution that
wishes to participate in this program as an "extended
care facility" (i.e., a skilled nursing facility) and to be
eligible for Medicare funds in that program, must meet
those standards. They also have an impact beyond
their technical application to Medicare-participating facilities, because they have a great influence, nationally,
on what is regarded as a proper standard of care for
any skilled nursing facility. For this reason, I would
urge that the consumer should expect a skilled nursing
facility to meet these requirements whether or not it
participates in a Medicare program.

It should be noted also that regulations have been
adopted, governing "intermediate care facilities." [4]
These are institutions which provide health-related
care to individuals who, because of their physical or
mental condition, need more than just custodial (room

and board) care but less than that provided in a skilled nursing facility. If you are confused as to the difference between the two types of facilities don't be discouraged; the courts have also had difficulty distinguishing between them. Ask the administrator of the facility in which you are interested to classify it for you, and act accordingly.

A skilled nursing facility must have professional personnel, including one or more physicians and registered nurses to govern the skilled nursing care and related medical services it provides. It must maintain clinical records on all patients. It must provide 24-hour nursing service with at least one full-time registered nurse. It must provide an appropriate plan for the dispensing and administering of drugs and medicines; it must have a proper utilization review plan and it must meet state licensing requirements. No resident or patient may be excluded from any of the benefits of the facility on the ground of race or national origin. The facility must have a full-time, qualified administrator, physicians available for emergency care, a dietary service supervised by a qualified dietitian, and a program of restorative nursing care designed to maintain function or improve the patient's ability to carry out the activities of daily living. Therapy programs must be run by qualified people. These are some of the fundamental standards that must be met under the Medicare regulations.[5] There are others, more detailed, and state requirements may be greater.

In addition, and just as significant, are a bundle of rights conferred by the federal regulations that are commonly referred to as the patient's "bill of rights." A skilled nursing facility must provide for these. They are as follows: [6]

Each patient admitted to the facility—

(1) Is fully informed, as evidenced by the patient's written acknowledgement, prior to or at the time of admission and during stay, of these rights and of all rules and regulations governing patient conduct and responsibilities;

(2) Is fully informed, prior to or at the time of admission and during stay, of services available in the facility, and of related charges including any charges for services not covered under titles 18 or 19 of the Social Security Act, or not covered by the facility's basic per diem rate;

(3) Is fully informed, by a physician, of his medical condition unless medically contraindicated (as documented by a physician in his medical record), and is afforded the opportunity to participate in the planning of his medical treatment and to refuse to participate in experimental research;

(4) Is transferred or discharged *only for medical reason* or for his welfare or that of other patients, or for non-payment for his stay (except as prohibited by titles 18 or 19 of the SSA), and is given reasonable advance notice to ensure orderly transfer or discharge, and such actions are documented in his medical record;

(5) Is encouraged and assisted, throughout his stay, to exercise his rights as a patient and as a citizen, and to this end may voice grievances and recommend changes in policies and services to facility staff and/or to outside representatives of his choice, free from restraint, interference, coercion, discrimination, or reprisal;

(6) May manage his personal financial affairs, or is given at least a quarterly accounting of financial transactions made on his behalf should the facility accept his written delegation of this responsibility to the facility for any period of time in conformance with state law;

(7) Is free from mental and physical abuse, and free from chemical and (except in emergencies) physical restraints except as authorized in writing by a physician for a specified and limited period of time, or when necessary to protect the patient from injury to himself or to others;

(8) Is assured confidential treatment of his personal and medical records, and may approve or refuse their release to any individual outside the facility, except in case of his transfer to another health care institution, or as required by law or third-party payment contract;

(9) Is treated with consideration, respect, and full recognition of his dignity and individuality, including privacy in treatment and care for his personal needs;

(10) Is not required to perform services for the facility that are not included for therapeutic purposes in his plan of care;

(11) May associate and communicate privately with persons of his choice, and send and receive his personal mail unopened, unless medically contraindicated (as documented by his physician in his record);

(12) May meet with, and participate in activities of social, religious, and community groups at his discretion, unless medically contraindicated (as documented by his physician in his medical record);

(13) May retain and use his personal clothing and possessions as space permits, unless to do so would infringe upon the rights of other patients, and unless medically contraindicated (as documented by his physician in his medical record);

(14) If married, is assured privacy for visits by his/her spouse; if both are in-patients in the facility, they are permitted to share a room, unless medically contraindicated (as documented by the attending physician in the medical record).

All rights and responsibilities specified in paragraphs (1) through (4), as they pertain to (a) a patient adjudicated incompetent in accordance with state law, (b) a patient who is found, by his physician, to be medically incapable of understanding these rights, or (c) a patient who exhibits a communication barrier, devolve to such patient's guardian, next of kin, sponsoring agency(ies), or representative payee.

At the time of this writing, similar regulations have been proposed for intermediate care facilities.[7] These regulations would specifically grant to each patient of such a facility the following rights:

(1) To be fully informed of his rights and responsibilities as a resident at the time of his admission to the facility, or at the time the facility adopts such rules or regulations; the receipt of such information is to be acknowledged by the patient in writing.

(2) To be fully informed at the time of his admission and during his stay of services in the facility, charges for such services, services not covered under the Medicaid program, and the facility's per diem rate;

(3) To be fully informed of his physical condition by his physician unless medically contraindicated; to be allowed to participate in planning his medical treatment; to refuse to participate in experimentation for research;

(4) To be transferred or discharged only for medical reasons, his welfare or that of other patients, or nonpayment for his stay (except as prohibited by Medicaid law);

(5) To be assisted and encouraged to exercise his rights as a citizen and resident, including freely voicing grievances and recommending changes in staff and services;

(6) To manage his own financial affairs;

(7) To be free from mental and physical abuse and restraints; restraints must be authorized in writing by a physician or in the case of a mentally retarded individual by a physician or qualified mental retardation professional;

(8) If mentally retarded, to participate in a behavior modification program only with the consent of his guardian;

(9) To have his personal, health, and medical records treated confidentially, and to be able to approve or refuse their release, unless he is transferred to another health care institution, or unless state or federal law authorizes their release;

(10) To be treated with respect and consideration and in full recognition of his dignity; to be treated and cared for in privacy;

(11) Not to be required to perform services within the facility that are not therapeutic and included in his plan of care;

(12) To associate and communicate with persons in private; and to send and receive unopened mail;

(13) To participate in meetings and activities of social, religious, and community groups unless his physician documents his determination that such participation would be medically contraindicated;

(14) To retain and use his personal clothing and possessions as space permits; and

(15) If married to be ensured privacy for spousal visits, and if both are residents to be allowed to share a room unless his physician documents his determination that such action would be medically contraindicated.

If the patient is incompetent, or if his physician documents his findings that the patient is incapable of understanding his rights, the first four rights enumerated above devolve to the patient's guardian, next of kin, or sponsoring agency.

State law and regulations may also provide similar safeguards for the patient. I would urge you to adopt the attitude that the rights enumerated are not something given to the patient by the facility. They are a description of the patient's status, honored in the law, which is to be respected by the facility.

Underlying the relationship between the patient and the facility is the common law standard of care imposed upon the facility. The skilled nursing facility is bound to exercise toward the patient such reasonable care as his known physical and mental condition may require. The degree of skill or care ordinarily exercised by other facilities in similar circumstances is also a standard of reference.

Access to the facility by visitors interested in the patient is another important protection. The regulations mentioned above would seem to require it. A good facility should provide it freely, but you should be aware of the fact that the legal system may be used to enforce that right if it should be unreasonably denied.

It should be recognized that enforcement procedure for these rights is still not clearly defined. Some commentators have suggested enforcement through demands by the consumer for decertification of the facility which denies these rights, for hearings before state licensing agencies, or class and individual litigation to enforce the rights by court order. I am confident that in time the system will learn how to respond to the need for enforcement procedures. In the meantime, individual demands based upon knowledge of the resident's basic rights need not await any change in the law, and making such demands may be the first step

towards assurance of an adequate remedy for everyone.

The Nursing Home Resident and His Doctor

In chapter seven the authors alluded to the problem
presented by the physician who seems to forget his patient after the patient's admission to the facility. Of
course, all the ordinary principles governing the standard of care that must be exercised by the physician
towards his patient apply equally to the nursing home
resident; that is, the law requires that a physician must
have and use, in the treatment of a patient, a reasonable or ordinary degree of skill and care.[8] Recently, in
determining what the ordinary degree of skill and care
is, the courts have begun to look at national rather
than merely local standards.

Diligence in seeing the patient or the extent of a
physician's obligation in severing his or her relationship with the patient are simply parts of the overall
obligation. Nevertheless, the law has given special attention to the problem of attendance by the physician
on his nursing home patient.

Federal regulations applicable to skilled nursing facilities provide that the health care of every patient
must be under the supervision of a physician who pre-
scribes a planned regimen of total care, based upon a
medical evaluation of the patient's immediate and long
term needs. Physician visits to review the patient's condition in the context of that plan are required once
every 30 days for the first 90 days after admission, and
thereafter changes in visitation must be specially reviewed.[9] State regulations may be more stringent. Beyond this, the courts which have considered the prob-

lem have also evolved standards which are applied to assess claims of malpractice if an injury has occurred as a result of a physician's negligence. These standards are generalities whose application depends on the facts presented in any individual case, but the following statement is typical: "A physician, in the absence of an agreement to the contrary, is, during the existence of the relationship of physician and patient, under a duty to give to his patient the needed continued care, and a lack of the requisite diligence on the part of the physician in attending the patient constitutes negligence or malpractice rendering the physician liable." [10] Of course, there is no liability, notwithstanding a failure of diligence, unless the patient has been injured.

The courts have also evolved the principle that a physician must continue his treatment of the patient and may not withdraw until:

a) The doctor and his patient (or the patient's guardian) end the relationship by mutual consent, or

b) The physician is dismissed by the patient (or his guardian) or,

c) The physician's services are no longer needed. [11]

A physician may also withdraw if he gives the patient adequate and reasonable notice, sufficient to give the patient time to secure other medical help. If these conditions aren't satisfied and the patient's condition is adversely affected, the physician may be liable for money damages. The point is, the nursing home resident who needs the services of a physician on a regular basis has the legal right to those services. Further, the facility, through its administrator, should assure that right. A continued and substantial failure to do so could be the basis of a demand for decertification, or of a claim of malpractice if an injury occurs as a result.

Wills and "Living Wills"

One condition must be met before either a last will and testament, or a "living will" (i.e., a formal declaration by a person that no extraordinary medical effort or expense is to be employed to prolong his or her life unduly) is valid: the person making the will must be legally competent. In the case of a last will and testament, a definition of the mental capacity that is a condition precedent to the validity of an ordinary will is expressed in typical fashion by the Maryland Court of Appeals, as follows:

"Whether a testator had sufficient mental capacity is determined by a consideration of his external acts and appearances. It must appear that at the time of making the will he had a full understanding of the nature of the business in which he was engaged; a recollection of the property of which he intended to dispose and the persons to whom he meant to give it, and the relative claims of the different persons who were or should have been the objects of his bounty." *Seller v. Qualls* 206 Md. 58 110 A.2d 73 (1954).

The casebooks are full of the unpleasant histories of will contests resulting from either well-intentioned or self-serving efforts to have a relative execute a will when the relative did not have the requisite competency, i.e., the mental capacity to make a will, or to change an existing will. Be certain that the nursing home resident is competent before you begin efforts to produce a will for him or her. I think it is also fair to say that no able attorney will draft a will unless he or she is satisfied as to the competency of the person involved. If there is serious doubt about the resident's legal competency to make a will, it is better to forget the will. A valid will requires much more capacity in the maker than the ability to hold a pen and to talk vaguely about the past.

The "living will" is of doubtful legal status. It is too new as a legal entity to predict what its effect would be in the event of a court challenge to its validity by a dependent spouse or relative. Nevertheless, if the nursing home resident is competent to execute such a document, the choice should be his. Contact the Euthanasia Council for more information about the ramifications of that kind of document.

In sum, there are ample legal resources available to protect the dignity and well-being of the prospective or present nursing home resident. A successful transition to his new lifestyle will be more likely if they are used.

SEVEN

Nursing Home Personnel and How to Get Along with Them

Mrs. Jones complained bitterly to her daughter about not having had any breakfast. "I'm starved," she whined. "I've had nothing to eat this morning. They never give me any food."

Indeed, Mrs. Jones did look weak and emaciated. When her daughter offered her some homemade pudding which she had brought as a special treat, Mrs. Jones gobbled it down as if she had never seen food before. The time was nine o'clock in the morning and Minnie's daughter Monica had stopped by for a visit on her way back from dropping her son at school. She often stopped at that hour and frequently heard the same complaint. The fact that her mother, even in her declining state, consistently complained about the same problem was disquieting. Monica was at a loss to know what to do. The week before, she had asked the pleasant nursing assistant whether her mother had had breakfast. The assistant verified that indeed breakfast had been taken to Mrs. Jones. Monica then asked whether she had eaten it. The nursing assistant did not know, for someone else had picked up the tray, probably someone from the kitchen. Mrs. Jones's daughter was becoming increasingly worried as the days passed by. She knew her mother had periods of confusion, but this was a daily complaint. Because of her family, she could not visit her mother earlier than nine to check on what was actually going on at breakfast time. Finally, one afternoon when Monica had brought the children to visit their grandmother, she saw a registered nurse on the floor. As Monica spilled out her fears and worries she found a very interested and sympathetic ear. She tried to be pleasant and courteous, but it was difficult. After all, it was her mother who was being mistreated. The nurse fortunately understood Monica's concern and said that she would look into the matter. They arranged to meet at the next visit two days later. The nurse found that a good hot breakfast was taken to Mrs. Jones every morning. Every morning it was picked up untouched. The solution was simple. Mrs. Jones, as often happens to elderly people, was slightly confused early in the morning and simply dozed through the breakfast hour. By nine or ten in the morning, when fully awake, she would be ravenously hungry, since supper had been served at 5:00 P.M. the evening before. She was often asleep by the evening snack at 8:30. The nurse held a meeting with the nursing assistants to explain the situation. Together they worked out a plan to be sure that Mrs. Jones actually ate breakfast. Most of the time this plan was followed, although there were a few slip-ups when a new nursing assistant did not know the routine. Mrs. Jones' daughter handled the situation very well. What would have happened had she not been there? How do we know that a nursing assistant will be responsive to questions? Look at the facts about nursing home personnel to find some guidelines for obtaining the best care for our relatives.

What is known about those who care for your relatives or friends in a nursing home situation? Who are these people? What approach is most effective and least threatening to them? What draws a person to seek work in a nursing home? What are the rewards in such a job? We think this information is basic to a realistic assessment of what to expect from this group of dedicated workers.

In a special report entitled "Nurses in Nursing Homes," published by the Subcommittee on Long-Term Care of the Special Committee on Aging, United States Senate, one finds the following description:

> It would be difficult to find in our society a working role more deserving of recognition and less recognized. We assign to this group of workers the role and functions of family members. They give care which relatives and friends are not available to give. We believe that most often they do it with gentleness and compassion. Yet we fail to define the role or develop it by means of even the most minimal requirements.[1]

What other pertinent facts does this report include?

1. Most nurses' aides [or nursing assistants] and orderlies [male nursing assistants] receive no training for their jobs; 53% of those applying have no previous experience.
2. Aides have little formal education; only one-half of the 280,000 United States aides and orderlies are high school graduates.
3. The turnover rate for aides is 75% a year.
4. It is very easy to obtain a job as a nurses' aide or orderly in a nursing home. References are seldom checked.
5. The pay is low. Starting pay is usually the minimum wage of $2.00 an hour or about $80 a week. The subcommittee reports further, "To dramatize the importance of these poor wages, our data show 38% of aides reporting themselves as the main support of their household. Job benefits are typically few, days off ir-

regular and include only one or two weekends a month."

6. The work is very hard, undesirable, and unpleasant. Few people relish employment calling for cleaning up after the abandoned members of society, many of whom are incontinent.
7. There is little hope for advancement. The chances for promotion are slim and wages will never get much beyond the minimum.

What are the actual duties of a nursing aide or orderly? What part of your relative's care do they perform? Here is a partial list of duties. (We say partial because the duties differ from home to home.) Basically these workers are responsible for feeding, bathing, grooming, assuring safety, and providing toilet care. They also make the beds, pass food trays, and provide fresh water. Most important are their observations of the resident's health and their performance of some preventive care including bedsore prevention. In other words, your relative will be dependent for all daily needs upon these hard-working people. To illustrate the kind of dependency which exists between assistant/orderly and resident, let us look at Mrs. Jones' schedule on one day in the nursing home:

6:30   Mrs. Jones is awakened for breakfast by a nursing assistant. Her bed is urine-soaked and is changed. This includes washing Mrs. Jones' back, buttocks, and between her legs. A clean nightie is put on and diapers are put in place.
7:30   Breakfast is brought by a nursing aide and fed to Mrs. Jones.
8:00   Vitamin pill and aspirin for arthritic pain brought by licensed practical nurse and given with a glass of water.

9:00   Mrs. Jones has moved her bowels in bed. Nursing aide removes soiled clothes and linen, and prepares resident for a tub bath. Draped with a towel for modesty, Mrs. Jones is lifted into the tub by an orderly. After being scrubbed by the nursing aide she must wait in the water for ten minutes until the orderly can be summoned. He removes her from the tub and the nursing aide dresses Mrs. Jones. Her hair is combed and teeth brushed. Mrs. Jones sits in a geriatric chair with other residents in the solarium.

10:00   An orderly whisks Mrs. Jones off to physical therapy and returns her to the same spot in the solarium a half hour later.

11:00   The nursing assistant checks Mrs. Jones for urinary incontinence. Finding her wet, the nursing assistant returns Mrs. Jones to her room and cleans her. Once again, the skin is washed and dried and the clothes are changed. Mrs. Jones remains in the geriatric chair for lunch.

11:45   Lunch, the main meal of the day, is served to Mrs. Jones. She can manage to feed herself at this meal if the food is cut properly by a nursing assistant.

12 noon   Aspirin for arthritic pain is given to Mrs. Jones by the licensed practical nurse. The medicine is taken with the juice on the noon tray.

12:45 P.M.   A nursing assistant puts Mrs. Jones to bed for an afternoon nap. Once again, her dress and diapers are wet. Her buttocks are washed and dried and a diaper put into place. The call bell is tied to the side rails of the bed. The rails are in the up position.

2:30   Nursing assistant gets Mrs. Jones up from her nap. She is not wet this time. She is placed in

her geriatric chair for the rest of the afternoon. The residents play bingo in the solarium. Volunteers run the game.

3:30   Mrs. Jones is checked by the evening staff for
urinary incontinence. The nursing assistant
finds her wet and changes her, following the
same routine as before. She is returned to the
geriatric chair.

4:00   Licensed practical nurse gives Mrs. Jones her
afternoon aspirin with a full glass of water.

5:00   Supper is brought to Mrs. Jones in her room,
and a nursing assistant sees that she eats it.

6:30   Mrs. Jones is put to bed for the evening by the
nursing assistant. She is washed and dried as
before because of incontinence. The nursing
assistant thoughtfully turns on the TV so that
Mrs. Jones can watch the evening news. The
side rails are up and the call bell in place.

8:00   The licensed practical nurse gives Mrs. Jones
her evening aspirin and offers her a glass of
juice with it.

8:30   The nursing assistant checks Mrs. Jones for
urinary incontinence. Finding her wet, she
washes, dries, and changes her. The entire bed
has to be changed at this time. Her teeth are
brushed and the TV and light are turned off.

10:30   Nursing assistant checks Mrs. Jones for comfort and to see if the bed is wet. It is dry.

2:00 A.M. Mrs. Jones puts on her call bell; her bed is wet.
The nursing assistant washes, dries, and
changes her. Minnie sleeps until morning.

In addition to the physical care she gives, the nursing aide provides emotional support. She endures with
great grace a constant chatter with the resident day
after day. Sometimes this conversation is enjoyable and
informative. At other times the conversation may be
demeaning, repetitive, hostile, and unpleasant.

Put yourself in Mrs. Jones' place and imagine how dependent you would feel. Remember, if the nursing assistant forgets to check the resident, Mrs. Jones will suffer and probably her skin will break down. Now put yourself in the position of a nursing aide doing her job. Imagine getting your children off to school (should you be on the 7-3 shift) and coming to work to face five, ten, or fifteen patients requiring care similar to Mrs. Jones'. It is hard not to imagine that 1) some part of the job might be overlooked, 2) the nursing assistant's temper might become frayed, or 3) the resident would feel neglected. We have not discussed here the role of the registered nurse in relation to the resident. She is primarily an overseer of care and a provider of emergency care. This would be true in intermediate or skilled care institutions. There may be no registered nurse in a custodial or personal care home. You may find a few nursing homes utilizing their nursing staff in innovative ways.

When putting this information into perspective two points become readily apparent: (1) It is a testimony to humanity that so much superb care is given to residents of nursing homes by untrained personnel, and (2) it is hardly surprising that situations such as Mrs. Jones' not eating her breakfast occur when care is provided by overworked, undertrained assistants and orderlies. There was nothing malicious in the provision of care for Mrs. Jones. The assistant did not know how to follow through.

What other personnel will be found in the nursing home? In part, the answer will depend on the requirements of the state and federal governments. The requirements are constantly being changed to be sure the best care is provided. At present in a skilled nursing home that is certified for Medicare payments, a registered nurse must be on duty twenty-four hours per day, every day of the week. The regulations for intermediate care and custodial care are less stringent. In rural areas where registered nurses may be in short supply, the regulations are somewhat less rigidly enforced. Your state Department of Human Resources can tell you the requirements.

At the very top of the pyramid you may find any variety of personnel combinations. A large Medicare-Medicaid certified institution will have a trained, licensed administrator at the top. Under his/her direction will be various department heads including nursing, housekeeping, dietary, pharmacy, social services, and recreational services. Smaller homes, especially those not qualified for Medicare-Medicaid payments, may not have such an elaborate structure. Some custodial homes taking a few residents are run by people who received their training through experience as nursing aides in a larger institution. Others may have a local physician in charge with nursing aides actually running the institution. The combinations vary greatly and the quality of care will depend, as always, on the concern and knowledge of the personnel.

Why do we elaborate upon personnel hierarchy? Simply to give you some idea of whom to approach should a problem or question arise. What route would you take to begin to solve a problem which was troubling your relative? How could you solve it immediately, before it gets out of hand?

1. *Gather the facts and take the time to try to put them into perspective.* Remember, in spite of the fact that it is *your* relative or friend that is complaining or suffering, there are always two sides to any question. Don't jump to conclusions; they are often wrong and then you have to soothe ruffled feelings.

2. *Find out who is taking care of your relative for the day.* If you don't know the nursing assistant, be sure to introduce yourself, identifying which resident is your relative. Ask the nursing assistant her name should he/she neglect to tell you. Always use the correct title (Mr./Mrs./Miss/Ms.) unless you are specifically requested to do otherwise. These assistants deserve your respect; you will usually get the same in return.

3. *Report the problem without prejudgment, and ask the assistant's opinion.* She may know the facts and solve it immediately. She may have to go to her supervisor for the answer. If this is the case, find out specifically when you will receive an answer. "Mrs. Smith, do you think you will have the answer for me before I leave in an hour?" On a busy day, and they all are, some problems are naturally going to be neglected. You have the right to a reply within a reasonable time and in accordance with the severity of the problem.

4. *Should no satisfactory answer be forthcoming, request to see the supervisor, be it the registered nurse, the licensed practical nurse on the floor, or the director of nurses.* Should the home be small you may have to go directly to the owner or operator. Whatever the steps necessary, keep as calm as possible and don't insult or threaten. Those personal wounds never heal and your relative may be the one to suffer.

5. *Should the problem entail a service outside of the nursing department, especially in a large home, ask the nursing assistant or supervisor how best to handle it.* You may, for instance, already be familiar with social services, or the dental department, etc. You may know exactly how to reach these people.

6. *Once again, we stress communication.* Listen carefully to all sides and be persistent in your follow-up. Your relative is not the only one living in the home, but you

are entitled to a proper and respectful answer to your questions.

7. *Be sure to thank everyone properly and sincerely as you go along.* A kind and appreciative word goes a long, long way towards ensuring good care for your relative. Let us caution you against trying to buy better care through extra monetary payments or presents. It is never right.

We will illustrate the preceding steps by discussing some of the more common complaints of elderly residents confined to a nursing home: brutality (either mental or physical, real or imagined), poor or inadequate food, and stealing of possessions. These problems require your attention, yet all of them require you to use insight and perspective. There will be innumerable other complaints that will require the same concern. The residents, remember, are all dependent to some degree for their survival on unknown people who are doing their best under difficult circumstances. *You are ultimately responsible.*

What would you do if you visited your relative and he not only complained of being hurt but also had a very large bruise on his right forearm? Your first reaction probably would be anger at the treatment, and a demand for an explanation and apology from the culprit. You might feel better, but that kind of action would accomplish very little except to put the staff on the defensive and probably eliminate any further communication between you, your relative, and the staff. This situation can be very disagreeable, frightening, and have long-lasting consequences. Instead, assess the situation. Try to find out from your relative how and when the incident happened. You may obtain a plausible story, a half-confused story, or no explanation whatsoever. With that information in hand, you have a duty to speak to the nursing assistant who is caring for your relative. Be sure you know to whom you are speaking. Be pleasant, yet concerned. If the assistant is comfortable speaking with you, she will probably share any information she has on the subject. The assistant, if she hasn't begun the daily care, may not even know about the bruise and would be pleased to have you point it out (nicely, remember). On the other hand, the nursing assistant may be aware of the situation, but feel unable to talk with you about it. Thank her for spending time with you and ask (with a smile) to speak with the floor supervisor. Follow the same routine up the pyramid until you are satisfied that you have all the facts. Sometimes these accidents happen when someone untrained moves the individual. It may be that your relative was frightened and was tense when moved. In older people, simply a tight grasp on the arm can cause a bruise. In addition, bruises in older people spread in the soft non-elastic tissue, resulting in a frighteningly grotesque appearance. In rare instances, a nursing home employee may actually hurt residents because of mental sickness of his own. Repeated complaints and bruises may be an indication that such is the case. Again, you have a duty to report any facts (and we stress facts, not hearsay) to the highest available authority.

Inattention to physical discomfort or emotional anguish occurs for a variety of reasons. This situation may be exacerbated by the condition of the resident and the quality of the personnel. Many situations necessitate a long, hard sorting of the facts before action can be taken. Let us use an example of a resident physically distorted because of arthritis, confined to a wheelchair, and given to chronic complaining. Imagine that this person is your relative and she complains that she never has clean bed linen. Your relative may take pride in being able to make her own bed with very little assistance. What plan would you follow in this matter? Maybe you will say to yourself, "It's a small matter," and pass it off. That is an easy reaction to a chronic complainer. Yet, you might say, "It is important to have clean linen. I wouldn't like dirty, crumpled linen myself." If possible, you could ask to see the bed and make a judgment as to the validity of the complaint. If it is not dirty, maybe your friend or relative has her days confused and thinks this is the day she receives clean linen. You can straighten out this situation by providing a good large-print calendar. Mark the days on which she is to receive clean linen. Suppose you find the linen in shambles. What do you do then? Ask the nursing assistant caring for your relative whether there is any reason why no clean linen is available today. Maybe the laundry is closed or there is some other simple reason. These situations do occur even in the best run homes. The assistant, trying to stay away from a complaining resident, has not passed this information to your relative. The assistants have feelings and it is natural for them to avoid a chronic complainer. Such a reaction is not right, but it does occur. Even some medical conditions can be overlooked in this manner. If you find some form of neglect in the care of your relative, assess the situation and then work your way up the hierarchy from assistant to supervisor as described above. Be patient and kind but forceful in righting the situation.

Meals are extremely important to many people confined to a nursing home. Food is a symbol of life and something regular to look forward to three times a day. As we saw with Mrs. Jones, she was well aware of the fact that she was hungry but unable to explain why.

The daughter was able through inquiry to obtain a solution to the problem. There are innumerable varieties of complaints about the food and the feeding of residents. When a nursing assistant finds herself with too many people to feed, she may skip trying to feed the desserts, bread, or salad. You may only hear about this situation from your relative. One solution is for you to arrange to be there at mealtime with your relative and help feed. Maybe you could arrange to eat with him. If you can manage this on a regular basis, do so and tell the nurses that they may count on you. Find out on what days they are shortest of staff. Someone else may get a better lunch that day as a result of the assistant not having so many to feed. It will do you no good to demand that he be fed everything every day if there are not enough hours for the staff to do this. Again you can alleviate pressure on the staff. Even though you are paying for the good care of your relative, you are the responsible party in the long run.

Mrs. Jones, you will remember, complained of thievery. Unfortunately thievery in nursing homes is not uncommon. Doesn't that infuriate you? You will undoubtedly feel hurt over the loss for your relative, and angry and furious at the home for allowing this to happen. How are you to approach this situation? First, get the story from your relative. Look everywhere in the room for the missing object. If the item is something that could have been left in another department, inquire about that. For instance, a sweater might turn up in physiotherapy. Should you not achieve satisfaction this way, then you must go to the staff. It is your duty to help protect your relative's possessions. Some stealing can be avoided by removing the temptation. Sometimes theft is committed by another resident. Many times families have approached us about lost items.

False teeth are commonly missed objects. Usually the resident, finding his teeth uncomfortable at mealtimes, removes them and carefully wraps them in a handkerchief or napkin. The napkin is left on the tray. The tray is picked up and taken to the kitchen. Anything disposable on the tray goes in the trash. Kitchen personnel do not check each napkin. The teeth are lost forever in the kitchen trash. Sometimes a favorite necklace will be on a bureau and another confused resident will wheel herself in and take it. This shouldn't happen, but realistically it does. It is a perfect example of a case where the staff could be mistakenly blamed. Beware of accusations until you positively know the facts. It can be dangerous and cause irreparable damage to your relations with the staff. If you do establish that there is thievery by the staff, go to the supervisor with the facts you have.

Let us implore you to bear in mind that you, as a relative or friend, are ultimately the most important person in being sure that proper care is given. You must retain that responsibility even after institutionalization. Many services will be provided that you cannot offer at home; however, you know the resident best and must see to it that you share the burden in concert with those who work in the institution.

Finally, what is the relationship between doctor, resident, and family within the nursing home setting? Before entering the institution, the resident probably felt secure in his relationship to a particular physician, group of specialists, or hospital outpatient clinic. Once a person enters a nursing home, these relationships may or may not continue. Some nursing homes have their own staff of physicians who will provide medical care unless you specifically request your own physician. Others expect you to retain your own physician although there may be a medical director attached to the home. Small personal care homes may or may not have a particular physician who takes care of the residents. State laws vary considerably in this respect. We advised in the chapter on nursing home shopping that the requirements and provisions for medical services be clearly understood. This understanding is important to a smooth transition from home to institution.

What can change in the relationship between physician and resident after institutionalization? It is said that physicians don't like to attend older persons in nursing homes, that they would rather treat more acutely ill patients, and that the Medicare-Medicaid requirements are too time-consuming.[2] This is not always true. We have known numerous examples of devoted care. We have also known residents who were, upon institutionalization, essentially abandoned by their physicians. The reasons for abandonment are unclear. Some physicians may think that the problem of visiting a resident in a nursing home is too much to fit into a busy day. The Senate Subcommittee on Aging reports that physicians don't like to be reminded of their own fate by going into a nursing home.[3] You may find that you have to face this problem. Should you be involved with a Medicare-Medicaid certified institution, the doctor must visit the resident every 30 days for skilled care recipients, and every 60 days for intermediate care recipients. The physician must write a note evaluating the resident's progress (or lack thereof) and sign any old or new orders. The quality of these visits varies. Some physicians will pay a very concerned, helpful, and reassuring visit; others drop in and out like the wind. It is well to be aware of these differences.

If you have medical questions, find out from the floor supervisor or other appropriate personnel when

the physician will visit. If you are the relative of a resident or the responsible party, be present at the time of
the visit if possible. Should you be unable to be there,
leave a note with your question and a request that the
doctor either call you or leave a written response. Be
succinct in stating the problem to the physician. He will
be pressed for time, but if you are reasonable he will
most likely be able to help. Often your requests on
medical matters can be answered by a registered nurse.
She should be willing to sit down with you and explain
any plan of treatment or therapy which you do not understand.

The legal and ethical implications of the doctor-pa-
tient relationship were discussed in chapter five.

The American Medical Association clarifies this relationship by saying that if the doctor does not give reasonable notice of termination and the patient thereby
suffers injury, the physician may be sued for abandonment. But a physician is not obliged to continue his
relationship with patients who enter nursing homes,
and failure to do so does not in itself constitute abandonment.[4]

If you feel and have proof that proper medical help
is not available, there are a number of actions you may
take after you have exhausted all the possibilities
within the nursing home hierarchy itself:

(1) Change doctors.

(2) Report the inadequacies in a Medicaid-Medicare
certified institution to your local Social Security office
and the state nursing home licensing authority (see Appendix).

(3) Report the attending physician, with written evidence, to the county medical society.

Let us add a word of caution here. If you as a relative or friend of a resident have doubts about the qual-

ity of care being rendered by the physician, be very careful before you criticize. The relationship between the resident and the physician may be either one of long standing or a personally satisfying one. Older people have a right to their own choices, and to demolish such relationships, no matter how questionable, may be very traumatic to the resident. Such an action represents one more loss for the older person which he may be ill-equipped to handle at that time.

Keep communications open with the physician if at all possible. Here is an example of reasonable versus unreasonable behavior. Return to Mrs. Jones, who is in a large, well-run nursing home. One day Monica visited and found her mother breathing very peculiarly. She seemed uncomfortable and restless. No one was paying any attention. Monica found the nursing assistant and asked if she knew anything about the breathing difficulties. Since it was early in the day, the nursing assistant had not known about the condition. Monica pleasantly asked her if she would call the supervisor. The supervisor did come and was able to verify that she knew of the change in Mrs. Jones' condition and that the doctor had been called. Monica remained with her mother until the doctor arrived and she saw that treatment had been instituted for what was diagnosed as pneumonia. In this situation the obvious proper steps were taken. Monica remained calm. She was now practiced in the ways of the medical world and had learned to be patient. Her calm attitude was very reassuring to her mother.

Monica could have become so concerned that she loudly demanded medical attention at once. This action seems only to put all those actually caring for a resident in a flurry. In addition, Monica could have called the doctor even though he had already been summoned. There may be instances when a relative is forced to use an extra nudge, but, with tact, help will usually be available much faster. One other consoling fact to remember is that a nurse can always send a resident to a hospital without a doctor's order if she thinks that the situation warrants it.

EIGHT

Death of the Elderly Nursing Home Resident

Our story of Minnie Jones, you will recall, ended with her death. The children remained at the bedside, loving, caring, and concerned until the end. Despite their concern for her, they couldn't fill her final needs. They, like many of us, were uncomfortable with the actual fact of dying. They had made one final decision. There would be no heroic life sustaining measures. This is a difficult area to agree on for the family and the dying. After making that decision, the children did their best by remaining with her. But it was a difficult time.

This chapter treats death as it inevitably affects us all. How can we prepare for death? What responses does imminent death foster in us? How can we most help the dying?

> Above all, even if the old person is struck by no particular misfortune, he has usually either lost his reasons for living or he has discovered their absence. When the world alters or displays itself in such a way that remaining in it becomes unbearable a young man can hope for change; an old man cannot. All that is left for him is to wish for death. . . .[1]

These remarks by Simone de Beauvoir indicate a desire on the part of the older person for death. Yet, fear of death can be just as strong a force tugging a person of any age toward life. Dr. Kübler-Ross says that we never imagine our own death and even view it in catastrophic terms.[2] How do these opposing forces interplay in the lives of the elderly as they approach the last stage of life? What part do family, friends, nursing home personnel have in an individual's life as it ends? What goals can be achieved before the actual time of death?

Doctor Kübler-Ross offers some guides for thinking about death. She suggests a way to identify the major needs and emotions of the dying person and those close to him. We see patients experiencing periods of denial, anger, bargaining, depression, and sometimes acceptance by the actual time of death. Some people experience all of them; some do not. The aging person meanders through these stages at a much slower rate than a younger person experiencing a terminal illness.[3]

> Old age is not an illness, nor is it an incurable disease.
> Nevertheless, the penalties and restriction imposed by out-
> living one's contemporaries mean that advanced old age
> often does take on the characteristics of a relentless and
> fatal illness.[4]

An institutionalized older person may well have begun this emotional journey before he or she was admitted. Certainly the admission itself to an institution means a beginning on this journey. Close friends and family may experience this same emotional journey with the elderly dying person. An awareness of the process is useful to understand the older person and to provide support for him.

Everyone in some way denies the aging process. In a society oriented toward youthfulness, denial of the ef-fects of normal wear and tear is pervasive. If an older person has denied his losses and limitations as they occurred, the process of entering a nursing home may be an enormous shock. Younger friends and relatives may not admit the disintegration of their friend because to do so requires them to face their own. Denial also supports hope. During this time, as in all stages of death, a person may experience periods of vacillation. Family and friends must listen with great care to the elderly. What are they saying? We have heard older people say one day, "I wish I could die," only to deny the next day that old age has had any effect on them and to talk cheerily about the future. In time, however, the older person usually begins to put his or her condition into perspective. As this process takes place anger may be expressed. Relatives, friends, and nursing home personnel may find themselves the target of this anger. It may be expressed in both words and actions. Why did Mrs. Jones refuse to speak with her children? Was she angry that the end was approaching? Why would an older person strike someone with a cane? It may be simply anger at a deteriorating condition. The use of bedrails at night is another familiar cause of anger. They remind the older person in the most threatening way of his helplessness. He wants to be alive and the bedrails may symbolize death and even burial.

The older person facing the end of life may bargain with his doctor, God, or whomever he thinks controls his life. He may bargain for just a little more time to accomplish certain things. If entrance to a nursing home represents part of this journey, this too may become a bargaining point. Bargaining, then, may be an attempt to prolong the inevitable. As the ability to perform certain daily tasks slips away, a person is bound to suffer periods of grief and depression. He can no longer deny the effects of age or disease. Anger has been spent and there is nothing left for which to bargain. Gradually the older individual must set new and smaller horizons as his physical and or mental state diminishes. Recall that Minnie Jones was able to accept the small losses as she coped with the aging process. She adjusted not only to the loss of her husband and friends, but to the slowing and loss of her formerly robust physique. She had inner resources and was very fortunate in having a supportive family. Only when her own health deteriorated faster than she or her family could plan for did the orderly process of death become confused. The family then was unable to support their mother in a rational way. Grief became paramount and acceptance of death was outside their grasp.

As we have seen, Minnie Jones was characteristic of many elderly people in nursing homes. Others range from simply slowing down to being completely bedridden. No matter what their mental and physical state, all people require support to face death with equanimity. The older person may talk about death or even wish for it. It is essential that we listen carefully to every word. Is life unbearable because of boredom, or pain, or a feeling of uselessness? Or has the older person reviewed his or her life, put his house in order, and accepted death? It is difficult for the immediate family to hear an older relative discuss his feelings at this stage. Sometimes the personnel at the nursing home will be more objective about what they hear. The nursing home personnel should keep in close contact with the family. But it is also the responsibility of the family to talk often with those who care for their relative.

What, in particular, can we do to make a person more comfortable during this final phase of life? Their needs fall into four categories: (1) physical, (2) emotional, (3) social, and (4) religious. These needs are not listed in order of importance, for what is important to one person may be less so to another. Once again, we would implore you to listen carefully to what you hear and observe.

First, let us discuss the possible physical needs of a person who is facing death. Is he comfortable and free from pain? If the person can no longer speak, you may have to work very hard to find out whether he is comfortable. There are ways of communicating. If the elderly person can comprehend, you can establish some way for him to answer any question you may pose. For instance, you can suggest that the person squeeze your hand in answer to a question, or nod the head, or blink the eyes. Use your ingenuity, take as much time as you need, and find a method that will work. Then, ask a question. "Mother, squeeze my hand if you have any pain. Do you have any pain, Mother?" By the same method you can find out any number of important things. What will you do with the information? If the need is for something which you cannot provide, be sure you tell the personnel on duty. Follow it up and make sure the needs are met. If pain is the problem, what should you do? You can tell the nurse on duty who may be a registered nurse, a licensed practical nurse, or a nursing assistant. Find out what will be done to relieve the pain. Usually relief will be forthcoming quickly. Should this not be the case, find out in a pleasant but firm way what is to be done. Has the doctor written an order for medication or will it be necessary to get such an order? Today, there is no reason for unnecessary suffering. Sometimes the cure for pain is something as simple as a change of position in bed. Examples of basic, but no less important, problems are hunger, thirst, need for a bedpan, heat, or cold. How can the difficulty be identified if the elderly person does not seem to comprehend? Two factors are of major importance in this situation. First, always assume that a person understands even if there is no obvious outward indication of this fact. There is no way for you to be sure that a person does not understand, and, in order to preserve his dignity, assume that he does understand. Second, we must guess his desires at this point. Watch for any expression in the face which would indicate discomfort. Pain is expressed sometimes by clenching of the fist or wiggling of the toes. You can discover simpler things like a wet bed or an uncomfortable position. Put yourself in the place of the helpless and the basic physical needs become obvious.

Let us discuss the second category, the emotional needs. Would you like to die alone? How terrifying if no one understood that you were facing death, so you had to face it alone! There is probably no other time in life when a person is so apt to be left alone. Yet it is a time when compassionate understanding is essential. Why is this last stage of life so often lonely? Death makes us all uncomfortable. We must not allow this fact to prevent our support for a dying person, especially a dying relative. What can we do? What is supportive? The most important thing is to be with the dying person when asked (not later, which is often too late) and to remain loving. Just holding the hand of the older person and saying nothing is often as comforting as anything that can be done. That act in itself shows love, care, and concern. Another component of emotional care is the willingness of family and friends to allow the older person to die. We have mentioned before that a person needs a reason to live and wants to feel useful. At some point before death, these responsibilities must end. As an example, it would have been unfair for Mrs. Jones' children to beg her to get better so she could help them with their own children or for them to make her feel they couldn't survive without her. There is a point at which demands can no longer be made. At that time the dying person needs you, but you, in turn, must be able to release that person from life's duties.

We mentioned previously that families often follow the same emotional journey as their elderly relative. For you to be able to allow your relative to die is an indication that you have shared his feelings in this way. We have often seen examples of very demanding families. We remember, in particular, one gentleman whose heart pacemaker had stopped. He had requested that another one not be inserted. Since he was over 90 this was not an unreasonable request. The family had concurred in the decision. However, they became increasingly demanding as the father continued to fail. The demands for the nursing staff to urge more food, to give some tonic to revive the resident, were very persistent and time consuming. The family members would also tell the old man that it was his duty to eat. He wanted to die. He had put his life in order, was pleased with it, and was waiting patiently and comfortably for death. The family, however, made these last few weeks miserable with their constant demands on him. They simply could not accept his death. How much better it would have been had the family sat quietly at his bedside comforting him.

The third set of needs are social. An older person preparing for death may indicate some unfinished business to which he would like to attend. An obvious example is the writing of a will. If it is awkward for you to become personally involved, seek outside help. In most states a will can be written or dictated and signed in the presence of two witnesses. If possible a lawyer should be hired to attend to this business. This subject was discussed in chapter six. The method chosen will depend upon the complexity of the estate, the ability to pay a lawyer, and the mental health of the individual. A person may wish to leave his or her body for research. In addition, should the physical condition allow, a person may want to leave eyes to the eye bank, or make some arrangement to help another by leaving some organ for transplant. This can easily be planned by using the Uniform Donor Card, which is a legal document in most states and is easily and freely available from the following:

> The American Medical Association
> 535 N. Dearborn
> Chicago, Illinois 60605

> Continental Association of Funeral and Memorial Societies
> 1828 L Street, N.W.
> Washington, D.C. 20036

Another topic you should be prepared to face, especially when dealing with those with chronic illness, is euthanasia. Literally this word (from its Greek origins) means EU—good, THANATOS—death, or good death. This word is often confused with mercy killing. They are in no way the same. As is explained by the Euthanasia Society, life-support measures need not be used to prolong the dying process in cases of final or terminal illness with intractable pain or irreversible brain damage. In addition, medication can be given in sufficient quantity to eliminate pain even if the amount required speeds death. The whole subject of euthanasia is emotion-laden and the subject of much public discussion. Everyone, including physicians, has his own opinion. Should your relative want to discuss the topic listen no matter what your own views are. It is his or her life, not yours. A copy of "The Living Will" may be obtained free from the Euthanasia Educational Council, 250 West 57th Street, New York, N.Y., 10019. This document has no legal standing to date. But because the subject is under constant discussion and re-evaluation by the courts, there may be changes. The "living will" simply states that the person signing it requests not to be kept alive by artificial means under the conditions stated above. This wish is stated in writing in advance of the time when the signee can no longer take part in decisions affecting his life. It is an expression of his desires while still of sound mind.

Again, we urge families to discuss these subjects long before the actual need arises; before the time for placement in a nursing home, or death, is imminent and emotions may be heightened. Remember, however, should such business not be settled, it is almost never too late. Late is better than never.

Let us look at another example of unfinished business. An older person may wish to resolve a disagreement with someone in or outside the family. As part of what Dr. Butler calls "life review,"[5] a person will often wish to right old wrongs. Possibly there has been a long-term feud with a member of the family or a business associate. The older person may request an opportunity to settle this dispute. By all means provide that chance even by letter or phone. A measure of serenity and final acceptance of death may follow the resolution of an old problem. There may also be a need just to see or visit with someone before a person feels free to die. Suppose, and this does happen, a husband

and wife are in different nursing homes and are unable to visit very frequently. Near the time of death, there may be frequent questions about the well-being of the spouse. Arrange a visit immediately if possible. The same situation may apply to a child, grandchild, favorite niece or nephew, or anyone of importance to the dying person. It is not unusual for someone to die quietly after such a visit. We recall one lady whose husband, for financial reasons, was in a nursing home nearby. The husband was quite confused; however, his visits appeared to be meaningful though upsetting to both. The family, thinking they were preventing upsetting situations for this elderly couple, went to great lengths to keep them apart. The wife continued to fail until it became obvious that time was of the essence. She was depressed and restless even in her near-terminal state. Because of the intervention of the nursing staff, the husband was brought to the wife's bedside, albeit belatedly. After a brief but comforting visit, the wife died within the hour. Her face betrayed the relief the visit had secured.

We mentioned in the chapter on admission to a nursing home that final funeral arrangements may be required before admission. If such arrangements have not been made the dying person may be concerned. The subject of funerals is personal and often neglected because most of us do not feel at ease in discussing it. Funeral directors can be very helpful, especially if you approach them well ahead of time. It will be very difficult to make decisions about what is actually needed and affordable if there is a crisis at hand. Another source of independent information available to all is the Continental Association of Funeral and Memorial Societies, Inc., Suite 1100, 1828 L Street, N.W., Washington, D.C., 20036. This organization has offices across the country and gives factual information on types of funerals, burials, and services available. This information is provided free of charge.

The fourth important need is religious. For the elderly, organized religion may have been important in daily life. For some, religion may be *the* most important part of life. The relationship will remain the same in death. Others may desire no religious support. We should respect others' opinions without interference. If there has been no formal church tie in the past, but the patient indicates a desire for one, find a clergyman. If you are unsure where to turn there are usually clergy who visit nursing homes on a regular basis. If the resident has made no contact with the clergy regularly visiting the home, there may have been a personal reason. Sound out the resident. It may be that our relative or friend had once turned to that clergyman and had been unable to develop a satisfactory relationship. Find out whether there is a religious affiliation. You can always call the nearest church or synagogue and request that a clergyman visit the dying person. Indicate that this person has requested such a visit. Be sure, however, that this is what he really wants and decide with your relative or friend what to do.

Once these four needs have been met the older person may even tell you directly or indirectly when he is going to die. It is difficult for relatives and friends but those who are caring for him may hear the clues preceding death. Some patients actually say good-bye to a favorite nurse. You, as family or friend, may hear about this after the older person has died.

What are your responsibilities to a nursing home after the death of your relative or friend? If your relationship with the nursing home has been good, you may feel quite a part of the life there. In addition, the personnel may have become quite attached to and involved with the deceased. Ask yourself, how would you feel if you had bathed and fed and talked with a person over a period of months or years? Wouldn't you feel a loss at the time of his death or perhaps have a deserted feeling? Attending personnel at all levels sometimes experience just such a grief reaction. They will appreciate the opportunity to tell you this and perhaps even shed a tear with you. You, in turn, may want to express your appreciation for their care. We think the best method of thanks is to write directly to the people involved, sending a copy to the administrator of the home. It is difficult and exacting work to care for the elderly and one of the rewards is to have family and friends take notice. Remember, the staff is there twenty-four hours a day, so don't forget the evening and night people whom you may not know quite as well. Letters of commendation should be sent as soon after death as is feasible.

If the experience in the nursing home has not been good, we suggest two avenues of approach. First, if there has been someone or something especially good, be sure to call attention to this and see that praise is given in writing as suggested above. Second, the inadequacies should be documented as they occur, and a letter sent to the accrediting or licensing organization in the state. If the home receives federal funds (Medicare-Medicaid) a letter should also be sent to the state certification organization. (See Appendix IV.) Copies of these letters should be sent to the administrator of the home. You may, by this action, spare someone else an unpleasant experience.

Notes
Glossary
Appendices

NOTES

Chapter 2.
Who Are the Elderly in Our Nursing Homes?

1. de Beauvoir, Simone, *The Coming of Age* (New York: G. P. Putnam's Sons, 1972), p. 26.

2. *Ibid.*, p. 26.

3. United States Department of Health, Education and Welfare, *Characteristics of Residents in Nursing Homes,* Vital and Health Statistics, Series 12, #19, p. 13.

4. The Commission on Population Growth and the American Future, *Population and the American Future,* The New American Library, Inc., New Jersey, 1972, pp. 97–101.

5. Department of Health, Education and Welfare, *Mortality Trends for Leading Causes of Death,* Vital and Health Statistics, Series 20, #16, p. 2.

6. United States Bureau of the Census, Census of Population:1970, Subject Reports: General Population Characteristics, Figure 35.

7. United States Department of Health, Education and Welfare, *Demographic and Economic Characteristics of the Aged,* Office of Research Statistics, Research Report Number 45 (SSA) 75-11802, pp. 88–89.

8. Klein, Wilma H., LeShan, Eda J., Furman, Sylvan S., *Promoting Mental Health of Older People Through Group Methods,* Mental Health Materials Center, Inc., p. 135.

9. United States Bureau of the Census, Census of the Population, Subject Reports: Final Report PC (2)-7E, *Occupation and Residents* in 1965, United States Government Printing Office, Washington, D. C., Table 1, p. 3.

10. Klein, LeShan, Furman, *op. cit.,* pp. 32–33.

11. United States Department of Health, Education and Welfare, *Characteristics of Residents in Nursing Homes,* Vital and Health Statistics, Series 12, #19, p. 13.

12. Subcommittee on Long-Term Care of the Special Committee on Aging, U. S. Senate, *Nursing Home Care in the United States: Failure in Public Policy,* November, 1974, p. 5.

13. United States Department of Health, Education and Welfare, *Measures of Chronic Illness,* Vital and Health Statistics, Series 12, #24, pp. 8–11.

14. *Ibid.,* p. 23.

Chapter 5.
Reactions to Placement

1. Kastenbaum, Robert, *New Thoughts on Old Age* (New York: Springer Publishing Company, Inc, 1964), p. 207.

2. *Ibid.,* pp. 207, 208.

Chapter 6.
The Legal Status of the Nursing Home Resident

1. 3 Am. Jur. 2nd Agency S54, 55.

2. "Validity and Construction of Contract Under Which Applicant For Admission to Home for Aged or Infirm Turns Over His Property to Institution in Return for Lifetime Care," 44 A.L.R. 3rd 1174 (1972).

3. 20 Code of Federal Regulations S405 et seq.

4. 45 Code of Federal Regulations S249.12 et seq.

5. 20 Code of Federal Regulations S405 et seq.

6. 20 Code of Federal Regulations S405.1121(k).

7. Volume 40 Federal Register No. 43, March 4, 1975.

8. 61 Am. Jur. 2nd Physicians and Surgeons S110.

9. 20 Code of Federal Regulations S405.1123(b).

10. "Liability of Physician for Lack of Diligence in Attending Patient," 57 A.L.R. 2nd 379 (1958).

11. "Liability of Physician Who Abandons Case," 57 A.L.R. 2nd 432, 439 (1958).

Chapter 7.
Nursing Home Personnel and How to Get Along with Them

1. *Nursing Home Care in the United States: Failure in Public Policy,* Supporting paper number 4, April 1975, pp. 370–371.

2. *Nursing Home Care in the United States: Failure in Public Policy,* Supporting Paper number 3, February 1975, pp. 329–330.

3. *Ibid.,* p. 330.

4. Letter from Veronica M. O'Hern, Office of the General Counsel, American Medical Association, 535 North Dearborn Street, Chicago, Illinois, 60610.

Chapter 8
Death of the Elderly Nursing Home Resident

1. de Beauvoir, Simone, *The Coming of Age* (New York: G. P. Putnam's Sons, 1972), p. 443.
2. Kübler-Ross, Dr. Elizabeth, *On Death and Dying* (New York: Macmillan Publishing Co., Inc., 1969), p. 2.
3. *Ibid.*, pp. 38–137.
4. Weisman, Dr. Avery Danto, *On Dying and Denying* (New York: Behavioral Publications, Inc., 1972), p. 137.
5. Butler, Robert N. and Lewis, Myrna L., *Aging and Mental Health* (St. Louis: C. V. Mosby Company, 1973), p. 44.

GLOSSARY OF TERMS

Nursing Home and Medical Terminology

Ambulatory: able to walk about unassisted.

Ambulatory with assistance: able to get about with the aid of a cane, crutch, brace, wheelchair, or walker.

Atrophy: a wasting of the tissues, organs, or whole body.

Bed-chair patient: one who cannot ambulate without the aid of another person, but is not bedridden.

Bedpan: a device used to allow a patient to eliminate urine and feces into a pan while remaining in bed.

Bedridden: confined to bed.

Blood pressure: the measurement of the pressure of the blood in the arteries. (Abbreviation: BP.)

Bowel and bladder training: a program of retraining the bowels and bladder to function so as to minimize or eliminate incontinence.

Catheter: a tube passed through the urethra into the bladder to drain urine; other names used are foley, foley catheter, indwelling catheter.

Cerebrovascular disease: condition related to the decrease of blood to the brain.

Chair bound: unable to get out of a chair without the help of another person; one who is not ambulatory with or without assistance; may also be referred to as a bed-chair patient.

Chux: trade name for a pad which is soft on one side and weatherproof on the other; used under incontinent patients or under draining areas of the body; they are disposable.

Chronic disease: a disease of slow progress and long continuance.

Commode: a portable toilet used in a resident's room and emptied by a nursing assistant or orderly.

Colostomy: an artificial anus (rectum); the bowel then moves through an opening on the abdomen into an especially built bag called a colostomy bag.

Coma: a state of unconsciousness from which one cannot be aroused.

Contractures: stiffening of muscles and joints.

Continent: able to control the passage of urine and feces; the opposite state being incontinent or unable to control the passage of urine and feces.

Decubitus-care: care of a pressure sore once it has occurred including medication, dressings, and proper positioning.

Decubitus ulcer: other names used for this condition are: bedsore, pressure sore, decubitus sore; the lack of circulation of blood to an area of the body creates a sore or ulcer; this condition is usually caused by pressure on an area from sitting or lying in one position too long.

Dehydration: lack of adequate fluid in the body; this is a crucial factor in the health of older people.

Disorientation: loss of one's bearings; loss of familiarity with one's surroundings; loss of one's bearings with respect to time, place (where one is), and/or person (who one is); the opposite of disoriented is oriented.

Drainage bag: a plastic bag used to collect urine from a catheter.

Draw sheet: a small sheet covering a rubber or plastic sheet used under an incontinent patient in bed or in a wheelchair.

Feces: the waste matter from food discharged from the body through the anus.

Femur: upper leg bone.

Fracture: breaking of a bone or cartilage.

Geri-chair: a wheelchair which cannot be self-propelled; it must be pushed by someone else; a tray is attached across the lap on the armrests of the chair.

Hand feeding: feeding someone who is unable to feed himself.

Hand rails: railings placed around tubs, showers, toilets, and on walls of halls to aid in steadying someone who is walking.

Hip pinning: a surgical procedure used to repair a broken hip.

Incontinent: see continent.

Inhalation therapy: treatment with oxygen or inhaled medicines.

Injection: the administration of medicine or other nutrients directly into the tissues via a special needle; sometimes referred to as I.M.

Intravenous therapy: nutrients or medicine given through a needle inserted directly into the vein.

Life review: a reappraisal of worth and redefinition of one's purpose in life.

Malignancy: uncontrollable growth of cells as in cancer.

Mouth care: brushing of teeth; rinsing of mouth.

Mortality: statistically it is the death rate.

Nasal-gastric feedings: feeding through a tube passed through the nose down to the stomach; used when someone is unable to take nourishment by mouth.

Osteoporosis: reduction in quantity of bone due to decreased mineral-protein components.

Patient care plan: a plan formulated by a registered nurse in conjunction with the physician for the care and rehabilitation of each patient to his optimum potential.

Peripheral vision: indirect vision.

P.O.: abbreviation used for "by mouth."

Private patient: a patient who pays for care out of own funds.

P.R.N.: an abbreviation to indicate that the medication is given or treatment performed only when the need arises.

Prognosis: the forecast or outcome of a disease.

Restraint: in the nursing home setting it most often means a protective device used to prevent a patient from falling out of bed or chair, i.e., a belt tied to a wheelchair or a jacket with straps tied to the wheelchair; a jacket restraint could be used to prevent a patient from crawling over the side rails of a bed; wrist restraints are another form although less commonly used in this setting; a physician's order is required for the use of restraints in a Medicare certified institution.

Senility: the physical and mental changes which occur with aging.

Sheepskin: a natural or synthetic skin of a sheep which is soft and used to protect bony areas such as elbows, ankles, coccyx, from rubbing on anything; a device used to prevent bedsores.

Special diet: a diet which adds or subtracts certain nutrients because of a medical condition; an example is a diabetic diet; sometimes such a diet is called a therapeutic diet.

Spinal discs: relating to the vertical column or backbone.

T.P.R.: abbreviation for temperature, pulse, respiration.

Turn Q 2.H.: a patient who is unable to move himself for a physical or mental reason must be turned to a different position every two hours; this is the abbreviation.

Unit dosage: a system of individually packaged drugs which costs more per unit but only for the drugs used.

Utility room: a room for emptying and washing bedpans and commodes; dirty linens may be stored there for short periods of time before being sent to laundry.

Utilization review: a plan for evaluation of the use of patient services in order to maintain a high quality of care; this is usually done by a committee of at least two physicians and other personnel.

Visual field: the area within which objects are more or less distinctly seen by the eye in a fixed position.

Vital signs: temperature, pulse, respiration, blood pressure.

Walker: lightweight frame held in front of person to give stability in walking; this device offers more stability than a cane.

Wheelchair: a chair on wheels which a person usually can propel himself.

Description of Staff Which May be Connected With a Nursing Home

Administrator: a person licensed to run a nursing home—one who has received training in monetary, legal, social, medical aspects of running such an institution.

Dermatologist: a medical doctor specializing in diseases of the skin.

Dietitian: an expert in the practical application of diet in prevention and treatment of disease. Registered by American Dietetics Association.

Director of Nurses: a registered nurse who oversees the nursing department including nursing supervisors, licensed practical nurses, nurses' aids, and orderlies. She writes their job descriptions, hires, and fires. The director of nurses writes and executes procedures and policies for nursing practice. Consulting with patients' families, physicians, committees, community groups are important aspects of her job. She is responsible for quality and safety of patient care.

Licensed Practical Nurse: one who has completed one year of instruction in a school of nursing or vocational training school. He or she is in charge of nursing in the absence of a registered nurse. An LPN often gives medications and performs treatments. LPNs are licensed (by qualifying examination) by the state in which they work.

Medical Director: a physician (MD) who formulates and directs policy for medical care.

Nurses' Aid: (*nursing assistant*), *orderly:* no training or experience is required. Training is acquired on the job or in a short program conducted by a nursing home or vocational school. In an ICF or SNF their work is under the direction of an RN or LPN. They wash patients, bring meals, feed patients, and generally give all personal care.

Nursing Home Operator: synonomous with Nursing Home Administrator.

Nursing Home Owner: this may be a corporation or an individual. In the case of an individual, he or she may also be the operator.

Occupational therapist; one trained to aid in restoring and retaining functions of extremities through making useful objects. These products are often made in a special room called O.T. or occupational therapy.

Opthalmologist: a medical doctor specializing in diagnosis and treatment of diseases of the eye.

Physical therapist: a person trained to retain or restore function in the extremities (arms, legs, shoulders, etc.) through movement, exercises, or treatments. These services are often provided in a special physical therapy room, often assisted by the physical therapist assistant. Physical therapists are licensed by the state in which they work, and often have a trained assistant.

Podiatrist: a medical doctor specializing in diagnosis and treatment of diseases, defects, and injuries of the foot.

Reality therapist: a person trained to help reorient the disoriented to time, place, and person.

Recreational director, or recreational therapist: a person trained to plan activities which will promote restoration to self-care and resumption of activities of daily living for all patients.

Registered nurse: An R.N. is a graduate nurse who has completed a minimum of two years of education at an accredited school of nursing. He or she is licensed by the state in which he/she works.

Social worker: a person trained to aid in the social problems of a resident's life, e.g. family, adjustment to institutional life, procurement of special services, etc. The social worker is in the department called Social Services.

Speech therapist: one trained to aid in restoring and retaining ability to speak.

Terms Used in Describing Nursing Homes and The Types of Care Provided

Custodial, Domiciliary or Residential Care: care which provides assistance with personal needs such as food, shelter, dressing, etc. This care depends on unskilled personnel.

Intermediate Care: personal care given by nursing assistants and licensed practical nurses, including some simple medical procedures such as special diets, self-medication, uncomplicated dressing changes, and injections. Such care is given in an intermediate care facility or ICF.

Skilled Nursing Care: comprehensive planned care incorporating rehabilitation and restorative services including such things as drug therapy, inhalation therapy, occupational therapy, or administration of intravenous fluids. Such care is given in a Skilled Nursing Facility or SNF.

Licensing: a license is required to operate a nursing home for one full year at a time. This means that the home has complied with state inspection standards (these standards vary widely from state to state). Each home should have a copy of the license available for viewing. To check the reliability contact your State Nursing Home Licensure Office (addresses included in the appendix).

Temporary or Provisional License: a license extended to a facility indicating that the home has not met the state inspection standards.

Certification: certification of a home is required for the institution to participate in the federally funded Medicare programs. Certification inspections are carried out by the state licensing agency. The reports, by law, are available for the asking, but the full report requires a written request. For the nearest Social Security Office look in your phone book under United States Government, or dial Information, 555-1212.

Proprietary Nursing Home: a nursing home operated for profit or a commercial nursing home.

Non-proprietary or Non-profit Nursing Home: a nursing home which is non-profit making and is usually run by a religious or fraternal organization.

Third Party Payment: payment for services made by an agency rather than the patient, his family, or other responsible person. Examples are Blue Cross, Medicare, Medicaid, etc.

MEDICARE–MEDICAID: ELIGIBILITY AND BENEFITS

	MEDICARE—PART A	MEDICAID	SSI *
Government regulator	Federal	State with some Federal funds	Federal
Level of Care	Skilled Care (must be a federally certified institution) SNF	Skilled Care—SNF Intermediate Care—ICF	Custodial Domiciliary Residential
Eligibility	Individuals entitled to Social Security, Railroad Retirement and some disabled persons. (1) Medically you require skilled care. (2) A doctor determines the need. (3) You must have been in a participating hospital for three days in a row prior to admission. (4) You must be admitted to the SNF within 14 days after leaving the hospital. (5) Admission must be for the same condition you were treated for in the hospital.	Individuals whose income is diminished to a level stipulated by each State. Physician must determine the need for care.	All those over 65— the amount paid depends on the total income.
Duration of Benefits	Full payment for 20 days; partial payment for an additional 80 days.	Unlimited	Unlimited

* SSI—Supplemental Security Income Program

MEDICARE—Part B—Voluntary insurance for those over 65. Coverage will help pay for doctor's bills, outpatient hospital services, medical services and supplies, home health services, outpatient physical therapy, and speech therapy. Monthly premiums must be paid.

APPENDIX I

Agencies of the Federal Government Concerned with Aging and Nursing Homes

Executive Branch: Department of Health, Education and Welfare

Office of Nursing Home Affairs—ONHA
Dr. Faye Abdellah, Director
5600 Fishers Lane—Room 17B-07
Rockville, Maryland 20852   Tel: 301 443-6497

ONHA coordinates all federal long-term care programs.

United States Administration on Aging—AOA
330 Independence Avenue, S.W.
Washington, D.C. 20201
Contact Special Staff for Nursing Home Interests:
Ms. Cenoria Johnson, Director, or Sue Wheaton   Tel: 202 245-6810

Any voluntary group working with or for the aging may seek guidance from the AOA. There are similar offices located in each state. Addresses for each state are included in this appendix. This office also coordinates Nursing Home Ombudsman Program (see appendix for list of offices).

Social Security Administration—SSA
Bureau of Health Insurance
601 Security Blvd.
Baltimore, Maryland 21235   Tel: 301 594-1234

Legislative Branch:

United States Subcommittee on Aging
Subcommittee on Long-term Care
Senator Frank Moss, Chairman
Room 3121 Dirksen Senate Office Building
Washington, D.C. 20510   Tel: 202 225-5364

This committee collects information, holds hearings, publishes reports on various aspects of long-term care. Write either to obtain information or to give information on any aspect of long-term care.

137

United States House of Representatives Select Committee on Aging
Subcommittee on Health Maintenance and Long-term Care
Representative Claude Pepper, Chairman
712 House Office Building, Annex #1
Washington, D.C. 20515   Tel: 202 225-3913

APPENDIX II

State Agencies Administering the Older Americans Act

(see appendix on Federal Government agencies engaged in long-term care)

ALABAMA

Commission on Aging *#	Chairman	Mr. Jesse T. Todd
740 Madison Avenue Montgomery 36104	Executive Director	Mr. Emmett Eaton
		(205) 832-6640

ALASKA

Department of Health & Social Services * Pouch H Juneau 99811	Commissioner	Dr. Francis Williamson
Office on Aging Department of Health & Social Services # Pouch H Juneau 99811	Coordinator	Mr. M. D. Plotnick (907) 586-6153

ARIZONA

Department of Economic Security * 1717 West Jefferson Phoenix 85007	Director	Mr. John Huerta (602) 271-5678

* Agency designated to implement Older Americans Act Programs.
# Unit responsible for day-to-day operations of the Older Americans Act Programs.

Bureau on Aging #	Chief	Mr. Lawrence W. Martin
Department of Economic Security		
543 East McDowell, Room 217		(602) 271-4446
Phoenix 85004		

ARKANSAS

Department of Social & Rehabilitation Services *	Director	Roger B. Bost, M.D.
406 National Old Line Bldg.		
Little Rock 72201		

Office on Aging & Adult Services #	Chairman	Mr. Luther Miller
Department of Social & Rehabilitation Services	Acting Director	Mr. Elmer Zelsman
7th & Gaines		(501) 371-2441
P.O. Box 2179		
Little Rock 72202		

CALIFORNIA

Health & Welfare Agency *	Director	Mr. Mario Obledo
926 J. St., Room 917		
Sacramento 95811		

Office on Aging #	Chairman	Mr. Archer Kirkpatrick
Health & Welfare Agency	Director	Mrs. Janet J. Levy
455 Capitol Mall, Suite 500		(916) 322-3887
Sacramento 95814		

COLORADO

Department of Social Services *	Executive Director	Dr. Henry A. Foley
1575 Sherman St.		
Denver 80203		

Division of Services for   Director   Mr. Robert B. Robinson
the Aging #
Department of Social   (303) 892-2651/2586
Services
1575 Sherman St.
Denver 80203

CONNECTICUT
Department   Commissioner Mr. Charles E. Odell
on Aging * #
90 Washington St.,   (203) 566-2480
Room 312
Hartford 06115

DELAWARE
Department of Health   Secretary   Mr. Earl McGinnis
& Social Services *
Delaware State Hospital   (302) 421-6705
3rd Floor—
Administration Bldg.
New Castle 19720

Division of Aging #   Director   Ms. Eleanor L. Cain
Department of Health
& Social Services   (302) 571-3481/3482
2407 Lancaster Avenue
Wilmington 19805

DISTRICT OF COLUMBIA
Department of Human   Director   Mr. Joseph P. Yeldell
Resources *
1350 E St., N.W.
Washington, D.C. 20004

Division of Services to   Chief   Mr. Curtiss E. Knighton
the Aged #
Department of Human   (202) 638-2406
Resources
1329 E St., N.W.
Washington, D.C. 20004

FLORIDA

| Department of Health & Rehabilitation Services * 1323 Winewood Blvd. Tallahassee 32301 | Acting Secretary | Mr. Emmett Roberts (904) 488-4797 |
| Division of Aging # Department of Health & Rehabilitation Services 1323 Winewood Blvd. Tallahassee 32301 | Director | Mrs. Margaret Jacks (904) 488-4797 |

GEORGIA

| Department of Human Resources * 47 Trinity Avenue Atlanta 30334 | Commissioner | Mr. T. M. Parham (404) 894-5333 |
| Office of Aging # Department of Human Resources 47 Trinity Avenue Atlanta 30334 | Director | Ms. Mary Kay Jernigan (404) 894-5333 |

GUAM

| Department of Public Health & Social Services * Government of Guam P.O. Box 2816 Agana 96910 | Director | Mr. Pedro Santos (9-0, ask for Oakland overseas operator 746-4158/2191/4438) |
| Office of Aging # Social Service Administration Government of Guam P.O. Box 2816 Agana 96910 | Supervisor of Aging Services | Mr. Ricky Naputi 749-9901 x 324 |

HAWAII

Commission on Aging * #	Chairman	Mrs. Shimeji Kanazawa
1149 Bethel St., Room 311	Director	Mr. Renji Goto
Honolulu 96813		(808) 548-2593

IDAHO

Idaho Office on Aging * #	Director	Mr. John McCullen
Statehouse	Assistant	Mr. David Mueller
Boise 83720	Director	
		(208) 964-3833

ILLINOIS

Department on Aging * #	Director	Mr. Kenneth W. Holland
2401 West Jefferson		(217) 782-5773
Springfield 62706		

INDIANA

Commission on Aging and Aged * #	Chairman	Mr. Sidney Levin
Graphic Arts Bldg.	Executive	Mr. Maurice E. End-
215 North Senate Avenue		wright
Indianapolis 46202		(317) 633-5948

IOWA

Commission on Aging * #	Chairman	Dr. Woodrow Morris
415 West 10th St.	Executive	Ms. Leona Peterson
Jewett Bldg.	Director	
Des Moines 50319		(515) 281-5187

KANSAS

Department of Social & Rehabilitation Services *	Secretary	Dr. Robert C. Harder
State Office Bldg.		
Topeka 66612		

Division of Social   Director   Dr. A. F. Bramble
  Services #
Services for the Aging   (913) 296-3465
  Section
Department of Social
  & Rehabilitation
  Services
State Office Bldg.
Topeka 66612

KENTUCKY
Department for Hu-   Secretary   Mr. Leslie C. Dawson
  man Resources *
Capital Annex,
  Room 201
Frankfort 40601

Aging Program Unit #   Director   Mr. Harold Mann
Department for Hu-
  man Resources   (502) 564-6930
403 Wapping St.
Frankfort 40601

LOUISIANA
Health & Human   Commissioner   William H. Stewart, M.D.
  Resources
  Administration *
P.O. Box 44215,
Capitol Station
Baton Rouge 70804

Bureau of Aging   Director   Mrs. Priscillia R. Engolia
  Services #
Division of Human   (504) 389-6713
  Resources Health &
  Human Resources
  Administration
P.O. Box 44282,
  Capitol Station
Baton Rouge 70804

MAINE
Department of Health   Commissioner   Mr. David E. Smith
  & Welfare *
State House
Augusta 04330

Office of Maine's   Director   Mr. Richard Michaud
  Elderly #
Community Services   dial (207) 622-6171
  Unit   and ask for 289-2561
Department of Health
  & Welfare
State House
Augusta 04330

MARYLAND
Office on Aging * #   Director   Matthew Tayback, Sc. D.
State Office Bldg.
301 West Preston St.   (301) 383-5064
Baltimore 21201
                               Deputy   Mr. Harry F. Walker
                               Director
                                           (301) 383-2100

MASSACHUSETTS
Department of Elderly   Secretary   Ms. Rose Claffey
  Affairs * #
120 Boylston St.   (617) 727-7751/7752
Boston 02116

MICHIGAN
Office of Services to   Acting   Mr. Ron Kivi
  the Aging * #   Director
3500 North Logan St.   (517) 373-8230
Lansing 48913

MINNESOTA
Governor's Citizens   Chairman   Mr. Cy Carpenter
  Council on Aging * #
Suite 204   Executive   Mr. Gerald A. Bloedow
Metro Square Bldg.   Secretary
7th & Robert St.   (612) 296-2770
St. Paul 55101

MISSISSIPPI

Council on Aging * #	Executive	Mr. Horace L. Kerr
P.O. Box 5136	Director	
Fondren Station		(601) 354-6590
510 George St.		
Jackson 39216		

MISSOURI

Department of Social	Director	Mr. Laurence L. Graham
Services *		
Broadway State Office		
Bldg.		
P.O. Box 570		
Jefferson City 65101		
Office of Aging #	Director	Mr. Jacques O. Lebel
Division of Special		
Services		(314) 751-2075
Department of Social		
Services		
Broadway State Office		
Bldg.		
P.O. Box 570		
Jefferson City 65101		

MONTANA

Department of Social	Director	Mr. Theodore P. Carkulis
& Rehabilitation		
Services *		
P.O. Box 1723		
Helena 59601		
Aging Services	Chief	Mr. Daniel P. Kelly
Bureau #		
Department of Social		(406) 449-3124
& Rehabilitation		
Services		
P.O. Box 1723		
Helena 59601		

NEBRASKA

Commission on Aging * #	Chairman	Mr. Donald Russell
State House Station 94784	Executive Director	Mr. Glen J. Soukup
300 South 17th St. Lincoln 68509		(402) 471-2307

NEVADA

Department of Human Resources * 201 S. Fall St. Carson City 89701	Director	Mr. Roger S. Trounday
Division of Aging # Department of Human Resources 201 S. Fall St., Room 300 Nye Bldg. Carson City 89701	Administrator	Mr. John B. McSweeney (702) 885-4210

NEW HAMPSHIRE

Council on Aging * # P.O. Box 786	Chairman	Mr. Philip Robertson
14 Depot St. Concord 03301	Director	Mrs. C. Monier (603) 271-2751

NEW JERSEY

Department of Community Affairs * P.O. Box 2768 361 West State St. Trenton 08625	Commissioner	Ms. Patricia Q. Sheehan
Division on Aging # Department of Community Affairs P.O. Box 2768 363 West State St. Trenton 08625	Director	Mr. James J. Pennestri (609) 292-3765

NEW MEXICO
Commission on   Chairman   Mr. Clifford Whiting
  Aging * #
408 Galisteo—   Director   Mr. Roberto Mondragon
  Villagra Bldg.
Santa Fe 87503   (505) 827-5258

NEW YORK
Office for the   Chairman   Mr. Garson Meyer
  Aging * #
New York State   Director   Mrs. Lou Glasse
  Executive Dept.
855 Central Avenue   (518) 457-7321
Albany 12206

New York State Office   Senior Field   Mr. Harold Scher
  for the Aging   Represen-
2 World Trade Center,   tative   (212) 488-6405
  Room 5036
New York 10047

NORTH CAROLINA
Department of Human   Secretary   Mr. David Flaherty
  Resources *
Albemarle Bldg.   (919) 829-2790
Raleigh 27603

Governor's Coordinat-   Executive   Mr. Robert Q. Beard
  ing Council on   Director
  Aging #   (919) 829-3983
Department of Human
  Resources
Administration Bldg.
213 Hillsborough St.
Raleigh 27603

NORTH DAKOTA
Social Services Board of   Executive   Mr. T. N. Tangadahl
  North Dakota*   Director
State Capitol Bldg.   (701) 224-2310
Bismarck 58505

Aging Services# *   Supervisor   Mr. Gerald D. Shaw
Social Services Board of
  North Dakota   (701) 224-2577
State Capitol Bldg.
Bismarck 58505

OHIO
Commission on   Acting   Ms. Jessie Bartlett
  Aging * #   Chairman
34 North High St.   Executive   Mr. Martin A. Janis
Columbus 43215   Director
                                            (614) 466-5500/5501

OKLAHOMA
Department of Institu-   Director   Mr. Lloyd E. Rader
  tions * Social &
  Rehabilitative
  Services
P.O. Box 25352,
  Capitol Station
Oklahoma City 73125

Special Unit on Aging #   Supervisor   Mr. Roy R. Keene
Department of Institu-
  tions, Social &   (405) 521-2281
  Rehabilitative
  Services
P.O. Box 25352,
  Capitol Station
Oklahoma City 73125

OREGON
Human Resources   Director   Mr. Jacob B. Tanzer
  Department *
315 Public Service Bldg.
Salem 97310

Program on Aging #   Coordinator   Mrs. Edward L. Hughes
Human Resources
  Department   (503) 378-4728
772 Commercial St.,
  S.E.
Salem 97310

PENNSYLVANIA

| Department of Public Welfare * Health & Welfare Bldg. Harrisburg 17120 | Secretary | Mr. Frank S. Beal |

Office for the Aging # Department of Public Welfare Health & Welfare Bldg. Rm. 540, P.O. Box 2675 7th & Forster St. Harrisburg 17120

Commissioner Mr. Robert C. Benedict

(717) 787-5350

PUERTO RICO

Department of Social Services * Apartado 11687 P.O. Box 11697 Santurce 00908

President   Hon. Ramon Garicia Santiago

Gericulture Commission # Department of Social Services P.O. Box 11697 Santurce 00908

Executive Director

Mrs. Maria Isabel Vazquez

(809) 722-2429 (overseas operator)

RHODE ISLAND

Department of Community Affairs * 150 Washington St. Providence 02903

Director   Mr. Fredrick C. Williamson

(401) 277-2850

Division on Aging # Department of Community Affairs 150 Washington St. Providence 02903

Chief   Mrs. Eleanor F. Slater

(401) 277-2858

SAMOA

Governor of American Samoa * # Office of the Governor Pago Pago, American Samoa

Special Assistant

Mr. Palauni Tuiasosopo (Brownie) Phone 9-0 (ask for Oakland overseas operator Samoa 3-2121)

SOUTH CAROLINA

Commission on Aging * # 915 Main St. Columbia 29201

Chairman

Mr. John Lumpkin, Jr.

Executive Director

Mr. Harry Bryan

(803) 758-2576

SOUTH DAKOTA

Department of Social Services * State Office Bldg. Illinois Street Pierre 57501

Secretary

Dr. Frithjof O.M. Westby

(605) 224-3165

Office on Aging # Department of Social Services State Office Bldg. Illinois Street Pierre 57501

Administrator

Mr. James V. Anderson

(605) 224-3656

TENNESSEE

Commission on Aging * # Room 102 S&P Bldg. 306 Gay Street Nashville 37201

Chairman

Dr. William E. Cole

Acting Director

Mr. Paul Duncan

(615) 741-2056

TEXAS

Governor's Committee on Aging * #	Chairman	Dr. Alton O. Bowen
8th Floor Southwest Tower	Executive Director	Mr. Vernon McDaniel
211 East 7th St.		(512) 475-2717
P.O. Box 12786, Capitol Station		
Austin 78711		

TRUST TERRITORY OF
THE PACIFIC

Office of Aging * #	Administrator	Orah Young
Community Development Division		Overseas Operator
Government of the Trust Territory of the Pacific Islands		9-0/2134
Saipan, Mariana Islands 96950		

UTAH

Department of Social Services *	Executive Director	Mr. Paul S. Rose
State Capitol Bldg. Room 221		
Salt Lake City 84102		

Division of Aging #	Director	Mr. Iver C. Moore
Department of Social Services		(801) 328-6422
345 South 6th East		
Salt Lake City 84102		

VERMONT

Agency of Human Services *	Secretary	Mr. Thomas Davis
State Office Bldg.		
Montpelier 05602		

Office on Aging #   Director   Mrs. Pearl Somani
Agency of Human
Services   (802) 828-3471
81 River St.
(Heritage I)
Montpelier 05602

VIRGINIA
Office on Aging *#   Director   Mr. Edwin Wood
830 East Main St.
Suite 950   (804) 770-7894
Richmond 23219

VIRGIN ISLANDS
Commission on   Executive   Mrs. Gloria M. King
Aging *#   Secretary
P.O. Box 539   (809) 774-5884
Charlotte Amalie
St. Thomas 00801

WASHINGTON
Department of Social   Secretary   Mr. Charles Morris
& Health Services *
P.O. Box 1788—M.S.
45-2
Olympia 98504

Office on Aging #   Acting   Dr. Roy Schiendelheim
Department of Social   Director
& Health Services   (206) 753-2502
P.O. Box 1788—M.S.
45-2
Olympia 98504

WEST VIRGINIA
Commission on   Chairman   Mr. Clement R. Bassett
Aging *#
State Capitol   Executive   Dr. Louise B. Gerrard
Charleston 25305   Director
                                            (304) 348-3317

WISCONSIN

Department of Health & Social Services * State Office Bldg., Room 690 1 West Wilson St. Madison 53702	Secretary	Mr. Manuel Cabella
Division on Aging # Department of Health & Social Services 1 West Wilson St., Room 686 Madison 53702	Administrator	Mr. Duane Willadsen (608) 266-2536

WYOMING

Department of Health & Social Services * Division of Public Assistance New State Office Bldg. West, Rm. 380 Cheyenne 82002	Administrator	Mr. Jeremy Wright
Aging Services # Department of Health & Social Services Division of Public Assistance & Social Services New State Office Bldg. West, Rm. 288 Cheyenne 82002	Director	Mr. James Hammer (307) 777-7561

APPENDIX III

Nursing Home Ombudsman Program

The Nursing Home ombudsmen are responsible for developing a process at the community level which will be responsive to complaints from residents or relatives of older persons in Skilled Nursing Facilities (SNF) and Intermediate Care Facilities (ICF). (See appendix on Federal Government Agencies engaged in Long-term Care.)

REGION I
George Molloy
Regional Liaison
Nursing Home Ombudsman
    Program

Office of Aging, DHEW Region I
John Fitzgerald Kennedy Bldg.
    Rm 2007
Boston, Massachusetts 02203
Tel: (617) 223-6885

CONNECTICUT
Jacqueline Walker
Nursing Home Ombudsman
    Program

Connecticut Department on
    Aging
90 Washington St.
Hartford, Connecticut 06115
Tel: (203) 566-2480 x 29

MAINE
Richard Michaud, Director
Bureau of Maine's Elderly

Department of Human Services
State House
Augusta, Maine 04333
Tel: (207) 289-2561

John Shaw, Director
Maine Committee on Aging

State House
Augusta, Maine 04333
Tel: (207) 289-2561

Cay Jensen
Linda Hubbard
Nursing Home Ombudsman
    Program

Maine Committee on Aging
State House
Augusta, Maine 04333
Tel: (207) 289-2561

MASSACHUSETTS
John J. Donovan, Director
Massachusetts Nursing Home
  Ombudsman Program

Office of Elder Affairs
120 Boylston Street
Boston, Massachusetts 02116
Tel: (617) 727-7275

NEW HAMPSHIRE
Robert V. Johnson
Staff Attorney, New
  Hampshire State Council
  on Aging

14 Depot Street (P.O. Box 786)
Concord, New Hampshire 03301
Tel: (603) 271-2751

Professor F. Dane
  Buck, Jr.
Nursing Home Ombudsman
  Program

Franklin Pierce Law Center
Mountain Road
East Concord, New Hampshire
  03301

RHODE ISLAND
Joseph R. Marocco
Nursing Home Ombudsman
  Program

Division on Aging
150 Washington Street
Providence, Rhode Island 02908
Tel: (401) 277-2858

VERMONT
Gwen McGrath
Nursing Home Ombudsman
  Program

Office on Aging
81 River Street
Montpelier, Vermont 05602
Tel: (802) 828-3751

REGION II
Arthur Wolfe
Regional Liaison
Nursing Home Ombudsman
  Program

Office of Aging, DHEW Region II
26 Federal Plaza, Room 4106
New York, New York 10007
Tel: (212) 264-4592

NEW JERSEY
Don Muzyk
Division on Aging

Department of Community Affairs
P.O. Box 2768
363 West State Street
Trenton, New Jersey 08625
Tel: (609) 292-3765

John Walser
Nursing Home Ombudsman
   Program

Office of Human Resources
  —Legal Services
Department of Community Affairs
363 West State Street
Trenton, New Jersey 08625
Tel: (609) 292-6262

NEW YORK
Robert Bosman
Nursing Home Ombudsman
   Program

New York State Office on Aging
855 Central Avenue
Albany, New York 12208
Tel: (518) 457-1909

PUERTO RICO
Anna Maria Carillo
Nursing Home Ombudsman
   Program

Puerto Rico Gericulture
  Commission
Hawayek Building, Stop 18
Santurce, Puerto Rico 00907
Tel: (809) 723-9432 or 725-8015

REGION III
Donald Clapp
Regional Liaison
Nursing Home Ombudsman
   Program

Office of Aging, DHEW Region
  III
P.O. Box 13716
Philadelphia, Pennsylvania 19101
Tel: (215) 596-6891

DELAWARE
Nick A. Kakaroukas
Nursing Home Ombudsman
   Program

Division of Aging
2413 Lancaster Avenue
Wilmington, Delaware 19805
Tel: (302) 571-3481

DISTRICT OF COLUMBIA
Karyn Barquin
Nursing Home Ombudsman
   Program

Services to the Aged
1329 E Street, N.W.
Washington, D.C. 20004
Tel: (202) 638-2674

MARYLAND
Dr. Matthew Tayback
Director, Office on Aging

State Office Building
301 West Preston Street
Baltimore, Maryland 21201
Tel: (301) 383-5064

Dorothy S. Soyle
Nursing Home Ombudsman
    Program

Maryland Office on Aging
State Office Building
301 West Preston Street
Baltimore, Maryland 21201
Tel: (301) 383-5064

PENNSYLVANIA
Richard Bringewatt
Division of Planning and
    Evaluation
Office for the Aging

Department of Public Welfare
Health and Welfare Bldg.,
    Rm. 506
Harrisburg, Pennsylvania
    17120
Tel: (717) 783-1849

Donna McDowell
Thelma Jacks
Long-Term Care Advocacy
    Program

Office for the Aging
Health and Welfare Bldg.,
    Rm. 506
Harrisburg, Pennsylvania
    17120
Tel: (717) 783-1849

Carol A. Delany
Director, Pennsylvania
    Nursing Home
    Ombudsman Project

133 South 36th, Rm 501
Philadelphia, Pennsylvania
    19104
Tel: (215) 238-7776

VIRGINIA
Kathleen Fisher
Nursing Home Ombudsman
    Program

Virginia Office on Aging
830 E. Main Street, Suite 950
Richmond, Virginia 23219
Tel: (804) 786-7894

WEST VIRGINIA
Becky Baitty
Nursing Home Ombudsman
    Program

West Virginia Commission
    on Aging
State Capitol
Charleston, West Virginia
    25305
Tel: (304) 348-2243

REGION IV
Thelma Langley
Regional Liaison
Nursing Home Ombudsman
    Program

Office of Aging, DHEW
    Region IV
50 Seventh Street, N.E.
    Rm. 326
Atlanta, Georgia 30323
Tel: (404) 526-2042/3482

ALABAMA
John A. Henig, Jr.
Nursing Home Ombudsman
    Program

Alabama Commission on Aging
740 Madison Avenue
Montgomery, Alabama 36130
Tel: (205) 832-6640

GEORGIA
Yolanda C. Owens
Social Services
    Coordinator
Georgia Office on
    Aging

618 Ponce DeLeon Avenue,
    N.E.
Atlanta, Georgia 30308
Tel: (404) 894-5341

FLORIDA
Anne T. Menard
Nursing Home Ombudsman
    Program

Department of Health and
    Rehabilitation Services
1323 Winewood Boulevard,
    Rm. 425
Tallahassee, Florida 32301
Tel: (904) 488-1391

KENTUCKY
Harold Mann
Aging Branch
Bureau of Aging
  Services

403 Wapping Street
Bush Building
Frankfort, Kentucky 40601
Tel: (502) 564-6930

MISSISSIPPI
Bill Jordan
Nursing Home Ombudsman
  Program

Mississippi Council on Aging
P.O. Box 5136
Fondren Station
510 George Street
Jackson, Mississippi 39216
Tel: (601) 354-6590

NORTH CAROLINA
Robert Q. Beard
Executive Director
Governor's Coordinating
  Council on Aging

Department of Human Resources
213 Hillsborough Street
Raleigh, North Carolina 27603
Tal: (919) 829-3983

Vince Lamont
Nursing Home Ombudsman
  Program

Governor's Coordinating Council
  on Aging
213 Hillsborough Street
Raleigh, North Carolina 27603
Tel: (919) 829-4261

SOUTH CAROLINA
Bill Bradley
Director
Nursing Home Ombudsman
  Program

South Carolina Commission on
  Aging
915 Main Street
Columbia, South Carolina 29201
Tel: (803) 758-2576

TENNESSEE
Tim R. Turner
Nursing Home Ombudsman
  Program

Tennessee Commission on Aging
S and P Building, Suite 102
306 Gay Street
Nashville, Tennessee 37201
Tel: (615) 741-3056

Melissa Jones
Nursing Home Ombudsman
  Program

201½ Perry Street
Elizabethton, Tennessee 37643

Vivian Reynolds
Nursing Home Ombudsman
  Program

Area Office on Aging
413 James Building
Chattanooga, Tennessee 37402

REGION V
Mel Braginsky
Regional Liaison
Nursing Home Ombudsman
  Program

Office of Aging, DHEW Region V
300 South Wacker Drive, 15th Fl.
Chicago, Illinois 60606
Tel: (312) 353-4695

ILLINOIS
George L. Stanton
Nursing Home Ombudsman
  Program

Illinois Department on Aging
2401 West Jefferson Street
Springfield, Illinois 62706
Tel: (217) 783-5773

INDIANA
Maurice E. Endwright
Executive Director
Indiana Commission on
  Aging and Aged

Graphic Arts Building
215 North Senate Avenue
Indianapolis, Indiana 46202
Tel: (317) 633-5948

MICHIGAN
Ron Kivi
Acting Director
Office of Services to
  the Aging

3500 North Logan Street
Lansing, Michigan 48913
Tel: (517) 373-8230

Doug Roberts
Director
Citizens for Better Care
Nursing Home Ombudsman
  Program

960 East Jefferson
Detroit, Michigan 48207
Tel: (313) 568-0526

Larry Fish
Director
Upper Peninsula Nursing
  Home Ombudsman
  Project

107 10th Avenue
Menominee, Michigan 49858
Tel. (906) 864-2985

MINNESOTA
Diane Justice
Director of Planning and
  Policy Analysis
Governor's Citizens Council
  on Aging

Suite 204 Metro Square Building
7th and Robert Streets
St. Paul, Minnesota 55117
Tel: (612) 296-2770

Judy Sivak
Nursing Home Ombudsman
  Program

Governor's Citizens Council on
  Aging
Suite 204 Metro Square Building
7th and Robert Streets
St. Paul, Minnesota 55117
Tel: (612) 296-2770

OHIO
Catherine Logsdon
Nursing Home Ombudsman
  Program

Ohio Commission on Aging
34 North High Street
Columbus, Ohio 43215
Tel: (614) 466-5500

WISCONSIN
Duane Willadsen
Administrator
Division on Aging

Department of Health and
  Social Services
1 West Wilson Street, Rm. 686
Madison, Wisconsin 53702
Tel: (608) 266-2536

David J. Krings
Nursing Home Ombudsman
  Program
Office of the Lieutenant
  Governor

GEF—Room 498
201 East Washington Street
Madison, Wisconsin 53702
Tel: (608) 266-8944

REGION VI
Anne Bayne
Regional Liaison
Nursing Home Ombudsman
  Program

Office of Aging, DHEW
  Region VI
1507 Pacific Avenue
Fidelity Union Tower Bldg.,
  Rm. 500
Dallas, Texas 75201
Tel: (214) 749-7286

ARKANSAS
Delores Martin
Nursing Home Ombudsman
    Program
Office on Aging and
    Adult Services

Department of Social and
    Rehabilitation Services
7th and Gaines
P.O. Box 2179
Little Rock, Arkansas 72202
Tel: (501) 371-2441

LOUISIANA
Janet Slaybaugh
Planning Officer
Bureau of Aging Services

150 Riverside Mall
Baton Rouge, Louisiana 70804
Tel: (318) 389-2171

Elaine Bennett
Nursing Home Ombudsman
    Program

Bureau of Aging Services
150 Riverside Mall
Baton Rouge, Louisiana 70804
Tel: (318) 389-2171

NEW MEXICO
Marjorie Goetz
Nursing Home Ombudsman
    Program

Commission on Aging
408 Galisteo
Santa Fe, New Mexico 87501
Tel: (505) 827-5258

TEXAS
William R. Thomas
Deputy Director
Governor's Committee
    on Aging

P.O. Box 12786—Capitol Station
Austin, Texas 78711
Tel: (512) 475-2717

REGION VII
Lila Waldrop
Regional Liaison
Nursing Home Ombudsman
    Program

Office of Aging, DHEW
    Region VII
Twelve Grand Building
12th and Grand, 5th Floor
Kansas City, Missouri 64106
Tel: (816) 374-2955

KANSAS

Richard G. Wagner
Kansas Social and
Rehabilitation
Services

Services for the Aging
2700 West 6th
Topeka, Kansas 66606
Tel: (913) 296-4686

Edward Taylor
Nursing Home Ombudsman
Program

Services for the Aging
2700 West 6th
Topeka, Kansas 66606

IOWA

Leona Peterson
Director
Commission on Aging

415 West 10th Street
Des Moines, Iowa 50319
Tel: (515) 281-5187

Diane Heins
Nursing Home Ombudsman
Program

Commission on Aging
415 West 10th Street
Des Moines, Iowa 50319
Tel: (515) 281-5187

MISSOURI

Don Whitehead
Missouri Office of
Aging

Division of Special Services
Department of Social Services
Broadway State Office Building
P.O. Box 570
Jefferson City, Missouri 65101
Tel: (314) 751-2075

Joseph A. Emanuele
Nursing Home Ombudsman
Program

701 East 63rd Street
Kansas City, Missouri 64110
Tel: (816) 333-7680

REGION VIII

Clinton Hess
Director, Office of Aging
DHEW, Region VIII

19th and Stout Streets, Rm. 7430
Federal Office Building
Denver, Colorado 80202
Tel: (303) 837-2951

COLORADO

Phil Nathanson
Division of Services
for the Aging

Department of Social Services
1575 Sherman Street
Denver, Colorado 80203
Tel: (303) 892-2651/2686

George Hacker
Nursing Home Ombudsman
Program

Senior Citizens Law Center
912 Broadway
Denver, Colorado 80203
Tel: (303) 573-9313

MONTANA
Rich King
Resource Specialist
Aging Services Bureau

Department of Social and
Rehabilitation Services
P.O. Box 1723
Helena, Montana 59601
Tel: (406) 449-3124

NORTH DAKOTA
Jo Hildebrant
Nursing Home Ombudsman
Program

Aging Services
Social Services Board of
North Dakota
State Capitol Building
Bismark, North Dakota 58505
Tel: (701) 224-2577

SOUTH DAKOTA
Nora Johnson
Nursing Home Ombudsman
Program

Office on Aging
Department of Social Services
Kneip Building
Pierre, South Dakota 57501
Tel: (605) 224-3656

UTAH
Ronald D. Hampton
Programs Coordinator

Utah State Division on Aging
345 South 6th East
Salt Lake City, Utah 84117
Tel: (801) 328-6422

REGION IX
Jack McCarthy
Regional Liaison
Nursing Home Ombudsman
Program

Office of Aging, DHEW
Region IX
Federal Building
50 Fulton Street, Room 204
San Francisco, California 94102
Tel: (415) 556-4814

ARIZONA

Lawrence W. Martin
Chief
Bureau of Aging

Department of Economic Security
543 East McDowell, Room 217
Phoenix, Arizona 85004
Tel: (602) 271-4446

Beatrice Thode
Nursing Home Ombudsman
  Program
Office of the Governor

1717 West Jefferson Street,
  Rm. 107
Phoenix, Arizona 85009
Tel: (602) 271-3786

CALIFORNIA

Loretta "Pete-e" Peterson
Nursing Home Ombudsman
  Program

California State Office on Aging
455 Capitol Mall, Suite 500
Sacramento, California 35814
Tel: (916) 322-3576

HAWAII

Renji Goto
Director
Commission on Aging

1149 Bethel Street, Rm. 411
Honolulu, Hawaii 96813
Tel: 60220—ask for—548-2593

NEVADA

John R. Kimball
Nursing Home Ombudsman
  Program
Nevada Division of Aging

Department of Human Resources
201 S. Fall Street
Carson City, Nevada 89701

REGION X

Ruth Ward
Regional Liaison
Nursing Home Ombudsman
  Program

Office of Aging, DHEW
  Region X
710 Second Avenue
Room 1490, Dexter Horton Bldg.
Seattle, Washington 98104
Tel: (206) 442-5341

ALASKA

Mr. Noel Smith
Nursing Home Ombudsman
  Program

Alaska Office on Aging
Pouch H OIC
Juneau, Alaska 99811
Tel: (907) 586-1653

IDAHO
Arlene Warner
Director, Nursing Home
  Ombudsman Program
Idaho Office on Aging

Department of Special Services
State House
506 North 5th Street
Boise, Idaho 83707
Tel: (208) 384-3833

OREGON
Rex R. Seindling
Deputy Coordinator
Program on Aging

Human Resources Department
772 Commercial Street, S.E.
Salem, Oregon 97310
Tel: (503) 378-4728

WASHINGTON
Mrs. Joette Northey
Nursing Home Ombudsman
  Program

Washington Office on Aging
Department of Social and Health
  Services
Mail Stop 45—2
Olympia, Washington 98504
Tel: (206) 753-3393

APPENDIX IV

State Nursing Home Licensure Offices

State Nursing Home Licensure offices inspect institutions to assure a basic standard of care for the resident. They issue certification for institutions that qualify for federal programs: Medicare and Medicaid. These regulations are standard throughout the country. In addition, they issue state licensure for all long-term care institutions. These regulations vary from state to state. Copies of all regulations should be available from these offices.

ALABAMA
Nursing Home Licensure Office
Bureau of Licensure and Certification
Alabama Department of Public Health
654 State Office Building
Montgomery, Alabama 36104   Tel: AC 205 832-3250

ALASKA
Nursing Home Licensure Office
Department of Health and Social Services
Health Facilities Certification and Licensing
Pouch H 06 G
Juneau, Alaska 99801   Tel: 907 465-3340

ARIZONA
Nursing Home Licensure Office
Arizona State Department of Health Services
Licensing Section Room 102
1740 West Adams
Phoenix, Arizona 85007   Tel: 602 271-5164

ARKANSAS
Nursing Home Licensure Office
Arkansas Department of Health
Hospital and Nursing Home Division
4815 West Markham Street
Little Rock, Arkansas 77201   Tel: 501 661-2201

CALIFORNIA
Nursing Home Licensure Office
Licensure and Certification Division
Facilities Licensing Section
744 P Street
Room 440 Building 9
Sacramento, California 95814   916 445-3281

COLORADO
Nursing Home Licensure Office
Colorado Department of Health
Health Facilities Division
Evaluation and Licensure Section
4210 East 11 Avenue
Denver, Colorado 80220   303 338-6111 Ext. 311

CONNECTICUT
Nursing Home Licensure Office
Connecticut State Department of Health
Division of Hospital and Medical Care
79 Elm Street
Hartford, Connecticut 06115   203 566-3893

DELAWARE
Nursing Home Licensure Office
Division of Physical Health
2634 Kirkwood Highway
Newark, Delaware 19711   302 368-6880

DISTRICT OF COLUMBIA
Nursing Home Licensure Office
Division of Licensure and Standards
Department of Human Resources
1118 22nd Street, N.W.
Washington, D.C. 20037   202 629-5983

FLORIDA
Nursing Home Licensure Office
Licensure and Certification Branch
Division of Health
Department of Rehabilitation Services
P.O. Box 210
Jacksonville, Florida 32201   904 354-3961

GEORGIA
Nursing Home Licensure Office
Standards and Licensure Unit
Department of Human Resources
Division of Physical Health
618 Ponce de Leon Avenue, N.E.
Atlanta, Georgia 30308   404 894-5137

HAWAII
Nursing Home Licensure Office
Hospital and Medical Facility Branch
Hawaii State Department of Health
P.O. Box 3378
Honolulu, Hawaii 96801   808 548-5935

IDAHO
Nursing Home Licensure Office
Licensure and Certification Section
Department of Health and Welfare
Statehouse
Boise, Idaho 83720   208 384-3261

ILLINOIS
Nursing Home Licensure Office
Illinois Department of Public Health
Health Facilities and Quality of Care
525 West Jefferson, 4th Floor
Springfield, Illinois 62761   217 782-5180

INDIANA
Nursing Home Licensure Office
Division of Health Facilities
Indiana State Board of Health
1330 West Michigan Street
Indianapolis, Indiana 46206   317 633-6890

IOWA
Nursing Home Licensure Office
State Department of Health
Division of Health Facilities
Lucas State Office Building
Des Moines, Iowa 50319   515 247-4115

KANSAS
Nursing Home Licensure Offices
Medical Facilities Licensure Section
Adult Care Home Program
Forbes A.F.B.
Topeka, Kansas 66620   913 296-2359

KENTUCKY
Nursing Home Licensure Office
Division for Licensing and Regulation
Bureau for Administration and Operations
Department for Human Resources
107 Bridge Street
Frankfort, Kentucky 40601   502 564-7960

LOUISIANA
Nursing Home Licensure Office
Louisiana Health and Human Resources Administration
Division of Management
Licensing and Certification Section
P.O. Box 3767
Baton Rouge, Louisiana 70821   504 389-6266

MARYLAND
Nursing Home Licensure Office
State Department of Health
201 West Preston Street
Division of Licensing and Certification
Baltimore, Maryland 21201   301 383-2517

MAINE
Nursing Home Licensure Office
Division of Hospital Services
Department of Human Services
State House
Augusta, Maine 04333   207 289-2606

MASSACHUSETTS
Nursing Home Licensure Office
Long-term Care Facilities Program
Department of Public Health
80 Boylston Street
Rooms 560, 530
Boston, Massachusetts 02116   617 727-2699

MICHIGAN
Nursing Home Licensure Office
Division of Health Facility Standards and Licensing
Bureau of Health Care Administration
Department of Public Health
3500 Logan Street
Lansing, Michigan 48910   517 373-0900

MINNESOTA
Nursing Home Licensure Office
Minnesota Department of Health
Division of Health Facilities
Licensing and Certification Services
717 Delaware Street
Minneapolis, Minnesota 55440   612 296-5422

MISSISSIPPI
Nursing Home Licensure Office
Health Facilities Certification and Licensure
Mississippi State Board of Health
P.O. Box 1700
Jackson, Mississippi 39205   601 982-6577

MISSOURI
Nursing Home Licensure Office
Bureau of Nursing Home and Licensing and Certification
Section of Hospital and Technical Services
Missouri Division of Health
Broadway State Office Building
Jefferson City, Missouri 65101   314 751-2552

MONTANA
Nursing Home Licensure Office
Bureau of Licensing and Certification
Division of Hospital and Medical Facilities
State Department of Health and Environmental Sciences
Cogswell Building
Helena, Montana 59601   406 449-2037

NEBRASKA
Nursing Home Licensure Office
State of Nebraska, Department of Health
Division of Standards
Lincoln Building

1003 "O" Street
Lincoln, Nebraska 68508   402 471-2946

NEVADA
Nursing Home Licensure Office
State of Nevada Board of Examiners for Licensing of Nursing
    Home Operators
P.O. Box 629
Carson City, Nevada 89701   702 293-4111

NEW HAMPSHIRE
Nursing Home Licensure Office
Bureau of Health Facilities Administration
61 S. Spring Street
Concord, New Hampshire 03301   603 271-2151

NEW JERSEY
Nursing Home Licensure Office
New Jersey State Department of Health
Division of Health Facilities Evaluation
Licensing, Certification and Standards
P.O. Box 1540, John Fitch Plaza Room 600
Trenton, New Jersey 08625   609 292-5764

NEW MEXICO
Nursing Home Licensure Office
Health Facilities Services Division
Health and Social Services Department
P.O. Box 2348
Santa Fe, New Mexico 87503   505 827-2807

NEW YORK
Nursing Home Licensure Office
84 Holland Avenue
Albany, New York 12208   518 474-5032

NORTH CAROLINA
Nursing Home Licensure Office
Licensure and Certification Section
Division of Facility Services
1330 St. Mary's Street
Raleigh, North Carolina 27605   919 354-6646

NORTH DAKOTA
Nursing Home Licensure Division
Division of Health Facilities
420 North 4th Street
Room 215
Bismarck, North Dakota 58505   701 224-2352

OHIO
Nursing Home Licensure Office
Nursing Home Program
Licensing and Certification Division
Ohio Department of Health
P.O. Box 118
Columbus, Ohio 43216   614 466-2070

OKLAHOMA
Nursing Home Licensure Office
Licensure and Certification Division
Oklahoma State Department of Health
North East 10th and Stonewall Streets
P.O. Box 53551
Oklahoma City, Oklahoma 73105   405 211-5116

OREGON
Nursing Home Licensure Office
Health Facilities Licensing and Certification Health Division
Department of Human Resources
P.O. Box 231
Portland, Oregon 97207   503 229-5686

PENNSYLVANIA
Nursing Home Licensure Office
Commonwealth of Pennsylvania
Division of Long-term Care
Health and Welfare Building
Harrisburg, Pennsylvania 17120   717 784-1927

RHODE ISLAND
Nursing Home Licensure Office
Rhode Island Department of Health
Division of Licensure and Construction
75 Davis Street
Providence, Rhode Island 02908   401 277-2566

SOUTH CAROLINA
Nursing Home Licensure Office
Division of Health Facilities and Services
South Carolina Department of Health and Environmental Control
J. Marion Sims Building
2600 Bull Street
Columbia, South Carolina 29201   803 758-5491

SOUTH DAKOTA
Nursing Home Licensure Office
Health Facilities Program
Division of Community Services
Pierre, South Dakota 57501   605 224-3364

TENNESSEE
Nursing Home Licensure Office
Department of Public Health
Division of Health Care Facilities, Quality Assurance Section
490 Capitol Hill Building
Nashville, Tennessee 37219   615 741-7883

TEXAS
Nursing Home Licensure Office
Department of Human Resources
Nursing and Convalescent Homes Division
1100 West 49th Street
Austin, Texas 78756   512 459-4201

UTAH
Nursing Home Licensure Office
Utah State Division of Health
Medical Care and Facilities Branch
Bureau of Medicaid Certification
44 Medical Drive
Salt Lake City, Utah 84113   801 533-6157

VERMONT
Nursing Home Licensure Office
Nursing Home Licensure
Vermont Department of Health
60 Main Street
Burlington, Vermont 05401   802 862-5701 Ext 81 or 28

VIRGINIA
Nursing Home Licensure Office
Bureau of Medical and Nursing Facilities Services
Virginia Department of Health
109 Governor Street
Richmond, Virginia 23219   804 786-2081

WASHINGTON
Nursing Home Licensure Office
DSHS—Health Services Division
Office of Nursing Home Affairs
Nursing Home Survey Section
529 West Fourth Street
Olympia, Washington 98504   206 753-5840

WEST VIRGINIA
Nursing Home Licensure Office
West Virginia Nursing Home Licensing Board
1800 East Washington Street—Room 424
Charleston, West Virginia 25305   304 348-3221

WISCONSIN
Nursing Home Licensure Office
Facilities Regulation Section
Bureau of Health Facilities and Services
Division of Health
P.O. Box 309
1 West Wilson Street, Room 400
Madison, Wisconsin 53701   608 266-3024

WYOMING
Nursing Home Licensure Office
Medical Facilities Services
Department of Health and Social Services
Cheyenne, Wyoming 82002   307 777-7276

APPENDIX V

Non-Governmental Organizations Concerned with Nursing Home Affairs

American Association of Homes for the Aging—AAHA
1050 17th Street, N.W. (Suite 770)
Washington, D.C. 20036   Tel: 202 347-2000

AAHA represents the non-profit nursing homes.

American Health Care Association—AHCA
1200 15th Street, N.W.
Washington, D.C. 20005   Tel: 202 833-2050

AHCA represents the proprietary or profit-making nursing homes.

American Association of Retired Persons—AARP
National Retired Teachers Association—NRTA
1909 K Street, N.W.
Washington, D.C. 20006   Tel: 202 872-4700

Membership of age 55 or above, either retired or still employed. Publishes a bi-monthly magazine called *Modern Maturity*. Sponsors workshops, volunteer programs at national and community levels.

The Gray Panthers
6342 Green Street
Philadelphia, Pennsylvania 19144   Tel: 215 848-2314

A very active group of people of all ages who are attempting to counter the stereotype of the aged person. Specifically they have a subgroup entitled Long-term Care Action Project. They have published a useful booklet entitled *Citizens Action Guide: Nursing Home Reform,* by Griesel and Horn, which can be purchased for $1.50 at the above address.

The National Caucus on the Black Aged
1725 DeSales Street, N.W.
Washington, D.C. 20046   Tel: 202 785-8766

This organization supports measures to improve the life of the
aged black person.

National Council on the Aging
1828 L Street, N.W., Suite 504
Washington, D.C. 20036   Tel: 202 223-6250

Research and services for the elderly are the major areas of work.

National Council of Senior Citizens—NCSC
1511 K Street, N.W., Room 202
Washington, D.C. 20005   Tel: 202 783-6850

NCSC lobbies for the needs of the elderly. It has been involved in
the initiation of the Nursing Home Ombudsman programs. Ms.
Marilyn Schiff has directed the pilot effort, and these programs are
now established in all 50 states.